BIG BIBLE SCIENCE 2

More experiments that explore God's World

ERIN
LEE
GREEN

CF4•K

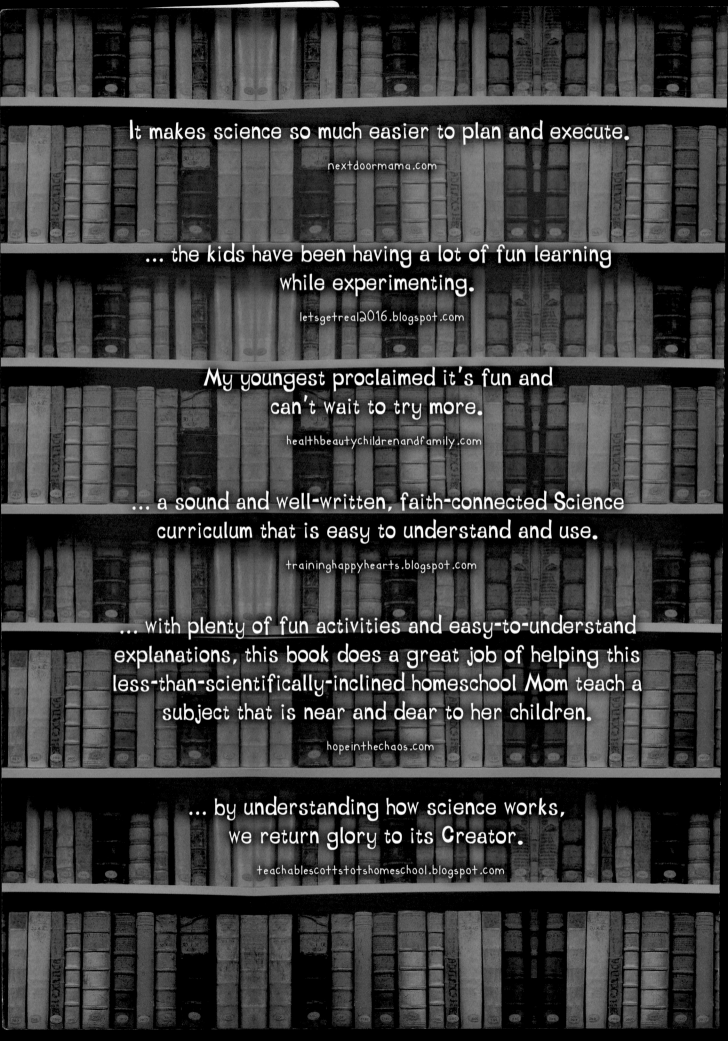

It makes science so much easier to plan and execute.

nextdoormama.com

... the kids have been having a lot of fun learning
while experimenting.

letsgetreal2016.blogspot.com

My youngest proclaimed it's fun and
can't wait to try more.

healthbeautychildrenandfamily.com

... a sound and well-written, faith-connected Science
curriculum that is easy to understand and use.

traininghappyhearts.blogspot.com

... with plenty of fun activities and easy-to-understand
explanations, this book does a great job of helping this
less-than-scientifically-inclined homeschool Mom teach a
subject that is near and dear to her children.

hopeinthechaos.com

... by understanding how science works,
we return glory to its Creator.

teachablescottstotshomeschool.blogspot.com

If you are looking for a science book that incorporates the Bible in a fun and exciting way for your young learners, then this is the book for you.

cumminslife.blogspot.com

... a fantastic resource for learning detailed science concepts through the light of God's Word. Scientific facts, biblical truths, hands-on activities, short biographies--this book has it all.

raisingleafs.blogspot.com

... a great addition to our homeschool.

loudmouthmomma.blogspot.com

Kids are naturally questioning the way the world around them works. Being able to talk about it with them while including how it relates to the Bible has been a great experience for us.

ourpieceofearth.com

This science curriculum is fantastic! It lines up with our biblical Worldview and I highly suggest it to Christian Homeschool families.

homegrownmotherhood.com

10 9 8 7 6 5 4 3 2 1

Copyright © 2019 Erin Lee Green

ISBN: 978-1-5271-0475-4

Published in 2020

by Christian Focus Publications Ltd.

Geanies House, Fearn, Tain,

Ross-shire, IV20 1TW,

Great Britain

Cover design and Page design by Pete Barnsley (CreativeHoot.com)

Printed in Northern Ireland by W &G Baird Ltd

DEDICATION:

This book is dedicated to my children,
who have taught me so much.
Special thanks to Ken Carpenter,
Paige Carpenter, and Ashlyn Ohm
for their expert critique.

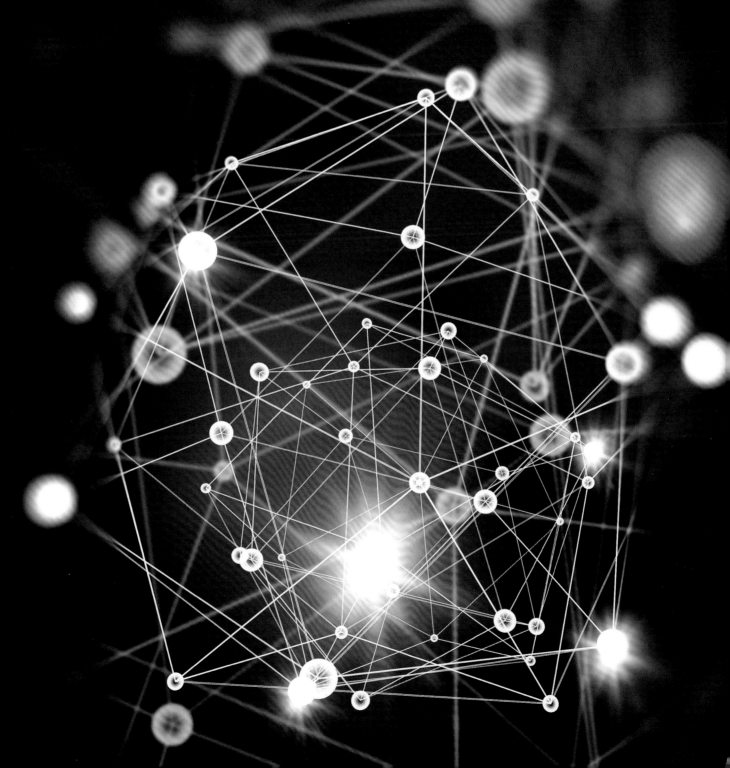

CONTENTS:

INTRODUCTION:

Each question your child asks is a teaching opportunity. Children are in a constant state of scientific investigation, with astonishing curiosity about the world around them. They naturally have scientific minds and questions. Their senses are bombarded with new experiences. Each time a young student learns a concept, his or her brain creates a neural pathway to integrate this new understanding. When the concept is repeated, the neural pathway is strengthened. The more this pathway is used, the stronger it will become. If it is not used, it can become lost. Every question is an open door to a potential new neural pathway.

God creates young minds to ask questions and seek answers. Ecclesiastes 3:11 reminds us, "He has made everything beautiful in its time. He has also set eternity in the human heart; yet no one can fathom what God has done from beginning to end." God writes His name on everything He creates. Children are designed to seek Him. It is up to teachers and parents to encourage our children to recognize God in the world. Educators should respond to students' questions with warmth and enthusiasm, help them discover, empower them to learn, and lay a firm foundation for a life-long relationship with God. Bringing students to love and worship Christ is the ultimate goal of Christian education. If you can show children God's creation, then you will inevitably bring them closer to Him.

But where to start in a world full of science that outwardly contradicts the Bible? Job 12:7-10 tells us to "ask the animals, and they will teach you, or the birds in the sky, and they will tell you; or speak to the earth, and it will teach you, or let the fish in the sea inform you. Which of all these does not know that the hand of the Lord has done this? In His hand is the life of every creature and the breath of all mankind." Science must be framed by the Bible, especially for the young learner. Although the writers of the Bible did not know about atomic theory or the carbon cycle, they understood that the natural world was God's good creation, a teacher of God's love, greatness, and mystery.

This book is designed to stir the imaginations of students and develop a lasting love for Christ.

The units are fun, interesting, and affirm the biblical worldview of creation.

The units are written to appeal to various ages and learning styles.

Homeschool families will benefit by encouraging older students to elaborate on the experiments, while younger students delight in the simpler activities.

Classroom teachers will enjoy the group activities and games.

Repetition of the various aspects of each unit is critical to form and reinforce new neural pathways and inspire a child to further curiosity.

HOW TO MAKE THE MOST OF EVERY LESSON:

TIMING

1

In order to enjoy teaching and learning these lessons, try not to rush. Move at a pace that is comfortable to your students. When attention spans wane, come to a stopping place and finish the lesson at another time. Take some time each day for about a week, repeating the stories and activities that hold the children's interest. Write science notebooks, practice memory verses, memorize scientific concepts, encourage further experimentation, and research the students' additional questions.

PRAYER

2

Begin each lesson with a prayer for God to open the minds of the children, help them concentrate, give the teacher patience, and for everyone to enjoy learning about His creation.

Leading a child to Christ is a blessed responsibility. Pray for your students, and be Spirit led for the right time to invite them to follow Him. Do not be troubled if you think a child is a bit too young or does not fully understand. In Matthew 19:14, "Jesus said, 'Let the little children come to me, and do not hinder them, for the kingdom of heaven belongs to such as these.'" If you have any concerns, seek the Lord and meet with a minister or church elder for advice.

MEMORY VERSE

3

Each chapter contains a highlighted verse that reinforces the science. Repeat the verse during the science lesson and in the weeks that follow. Memorizing Scripture is important for lasting change in Christians. Memory verses fortify our spirits and prepare us for the future.

BIG BIBLE SCIENCE 2

CHAPTER COMPONENTS:

OBJECTIVES:

These are simply stated science learning goals. They are for the teacher to get a quick survey of the lesson.

MATERIALS AND PREPARATION:

Decide on an appropriate location before beginning the lesson.

Many of the experiments are designed to be performed outside, in a wooded area or on a playground.

Gather the needed materials listed at the beginning of each lesson. The materials throughout the book are chosen to keep costs low. Most of the items are readily available in the average home or classroom, although a trip to the store will occasionally be necessary.

Always have a Bible nearby.

THE BIG IDEA:

This is a scientific explanation of the lesson. It ties in a biblical perspective and a memory verse as it introduces the lesson.

The length of the Big Idea sections vary depending on the complexity of the concepts and the intensity of the Bible lesson.

The Big Idea section should be completed before beginning the activities. In many cases, it may be beneficial to review the Big Idea during or after the activities are completed.

ACTIVITIES:

Some activities reinforce the biblical perspective of the lesson, but most are scientific demonstrations, games, and experiments.

In most chapters, the order of the activities is not critical.

APPLY IT:

Here you have ideas about how to look for examples of the lesson around the world. Reinforcing the key aspects of the scientific and biblical principles is key for students to retain the information.

GO BEYOND:

This section will challenge more advanced students to think and experiment further.

SAFETY FIRST

The Science in this book is quite harmless. However, listed below are some safety issues that may arise.

FALL RISKS

- Use teacher/parent discretion regarding child safety on playground equipment.

- Use caution when walking around a dark or poorly lit room. Make sure the room is clear of obstacles before turning off the lights.

DROWNING RISKS

- Supervise children around water. Children are drawn to play in water and explore its properties. However, drowning is a serious danger. Swimming pools, lakes, bathtubs, and even buckets can be hazardous.

INJURY RISKS

- Playground equipment is designed for maximum safety. Manage students' behavior appropriately.

  - Seesaws can result in serious injury if children jump off or touch moving parts. Use caution when getting on and off a seesaw.

- Tools (like knives, hammers and screwdrivers) have inherent risks. Use proper judgment regarding whether a child is old enough to safely handle a tool. Teach children proper use and demonstrate before beginning the activity. Wear safety glasses and gloves when appropriate.

- Exercise machines are notoriously dangerous. They can crush hands or fingers in the many moving parts. Instruct children to keep their hands behind their backs unless they are under direct adult supervision, participating in the activity.

- Watch for hazards when going for nature walks. Wear insect repellent and dress appropriately for the weather. If you are in an unfamiliar area, take precautions to not get lost.

- Wear safety goggles if a hairdryer is in use. Do not point a hairdryer at another person's face.

BURN RISKS

- Burn risks occur any time fire or heat is used. Keep matches and lighters out of reach of children. Always strike matches away from your body. Run smoldering match sticks under water before disposing of them. Coach children to keep their hands and faces away from candles and matches. Never leave a candle burning unattended.

- Supervise children vigilantly around kitchen appliances and cooking of any kind. Never allow a child to operate a stove. Keep cookware handles turned inward, out of reach. Keep hands and face clear of steam, as it can cause severe burns.

- Do not allow children to eat hot foods or drink hot beverages; let the food and drink cool first.

CHEMICAL RISKS

- Keep hands away from face when handling chemicals. Wash hands thoroughly with soap and water after the experiment.

- Vinegar is the most caustic chemical used in this book. Safety goggles are a good idea any time a chemical is handled. Do not breathe the fumes from a chemical. If you get a chemical in your eye, rinse thoroughly for at least fifteen minutes. See a doctor if irritation persists.

- For more details, the MSDS (Material Safety Data Sheet) for any chemical is available online:

  - Vinegar

  - Baking Soda

  - Hydrogen Peroxide

(Source: The Mayo Clinic)

MISCELLANEOUS

- Wash hands with plenty of soap and warm water after handling meat or bones.

- Children with cochlear implants should not perform any activities involving static electricity.

- The anatomy unit calls for physical contact and touching as various body parts are studied. Make sure all touching is on safe places on the child's body, never on the buttocks, breasts, or groin. Keep clothing ON for all lessons.

If you are a student using this book without an adult, the exploration aspect of each lesson will be even more fulfilling as you will be free to pursue and experiment on your own terms at your own pace. However, you will not be able to complete may of the activities that require a group of students. In order to make the most of science, you need at least one partner available whenever an activity calls for assistance. There are a few activities you should not do because they are not safe without an adult.

CHAPTER	ACTIVITIES A STUDENT CAN DO ALONE:	ACTIVITIES THAT REQUIRE ONE OR MORE PARTNERS:	ACTIVITIES A STUDENT CANNOT / SHOULD NOT DO WITHOUT AN ADULT:
Potential and Kinetic Energy	Slide Energy from God	Swing Spring Rider	
Simple Machines in a playground	Simple Machine Hunt Blessing Jar		
Mechanical Advantage of a Lever	Heavy Lifting Balancing Penny Act	Seesaw Opposites	Go Beyond: Drive a Nail
Fixed Pully: Changing the Direction of Force	Build a Simple Fixed Pulley	Movable Pulley Tug-of-War	Go Beyond: Exercise machines
Angular Momentum and Centripetal Motion	God's Love Möbius Circle	Swing & Angular Momentum Inertia	Swinging a Bucket Full of Water
Buoyancy of Boats	Water Displacement Boat Float Sink the Boat		Apply it: Get into a Swimming Pool
Law of Conservation of Matter	Giant Oak		Production of a Gas
Indications of a Chemical Reaction	Clean a Penny		Plaster of Paris Candle Baking Soda and Vinegar Hydrogen Peroxide & Yeast Mentos and Diet Coke

CHAPTER	ACTIVITIES A STUDENT CAN DO ALONE:	ACTIVITIES THAT REQUIRE ONE OR MORE PARTNERS:	ACTIVITIES A STUDENT CANNOT / SHOULD NOT DO WITHOUT AN ADULT:
Heat Capacity and Specific Heat			Heat Capacity Specific Heat Hot Chocolate Go Beyond: How Much Heat can it Hold
Condensation	Bottle in a Bag Cup Trap		
Colligative Properties	Freezing Point Depression More Science: Osmotic Pressure		Boiling Point Elevation
Symmetry in Nature	Linear Symmetry Butterfly Radial Symmetry Flowers		Nature Walk
Deciduous and Evergreen Trees	Tree Identification		
Plant a Bean	Bean Sprouting Sensing Gravity		
Parts of a Plant at the Dinner Table	Study the Food		Prepare and Eat the Food
Symbiosis	Matching Hints		Nature Walk
Bird Population Study	Build a Bird Feeder Bird Craft Bird Count Bar Graph		
Endoskeleton Versus Exoskeleton	Search for Creatures God's Creatures		Nature Walk
Carnivores, Herbivores, & Omnivores: Food Chain	Compare and Contrast Food Chain	Food Web	
How the Moon Shines	Lunar Reflection Starry Night Art Project	Lunar Reflection Lost-and-Found	
Weathering and Erosion	Mechanical Weathering by Pressure Mechanical Weathering by Freezing Expansion		Chemical Weathering by Acid Erosion by Wind / Erosion by Water, Particle Size Comparison Sinkholes & Chemical Weathering

NOTEBOOKING:

It is important to develop good habits of science and encourage sound thinking. A science notebook is a simple way of keeping records of inquiry based observations, experiments, and activities. It is an excellent communication tool for the teacher to access understanding and provide feedback. Notebooks are also an uncomplicated method for integrating math and literacy into a science curriculum. For younger or struggling students, the teacher can model data tables and notebook entries. Older or more advanced students can challenge their minds to organize their own thoughts. A science notebook can be used in multiple scenarios: when the student performs a teacher-guided activity as from this book, observes a natural phenomenon on his/her own, and designs his/her own experiment. A couple of good books to introduce the importance of keeping a science notebook are *Galileo's Journal, 1606-1610* by Jeanne Pattenati and Paolo Rui and *My Season with Penguins: An Antarctic Journal* by Sophie Webb.

GOOD NOTEBOOK HABITS FOR A YOUNG SCIENTIST:

- Use a notebook with stitched binding so pages do not fall out. A simple composition notebook works well. There is no need for the carbon copy type laboratory notebook. Write your full name and the year on the front of the notebook. Write more contact information on the inside of the front cover.

- Use non-water soluble ink. The teacher should use discretion as many children should probably bend this rule and use good graphite pencils, but please do not let them erase. Colored drawings should be done in crayon or colored pencil. Drawings and labeled diagrams are a wonderful way for young children to record data and observations.

- A science notebook is a documentation of facts. It is NOT a diary or record of opinions.

- Starting on the first page, number the fronts of the pages of the notebook. You may need to help your child with this. Devote the first two pages to "Table of Contents," with two columns: one for the name of the experiment, and one for the page number on which it begins. Construct the table of contents as experiments are completed.

- Never tear out a page. You could lose important data and injure your notebook. If a page is skipped, simply draw a single diagonal line across it. If an experiment is concluded before the bottom of a page, draw a diagonal line across the remainder of the page as an indication that it was intentionally left blank.

- Write on the fronts of pages only. Save the backs for sketches, quick notes, photographs, teacher notes, and calculations.

- If you make a mistake, do not erase it, scribble it out, or use White Out. Even if it is a spelling error or a wrong number, just draw a single thin line through the error. So much of the science we now know is correct, was originally thought to be a mistake.

- Use glue, instead of tape, to attach any photographs, data tables, or actual scientific evidence such as leaves or coins.

A science notebook entry for an early elementary age child may contain the following parts:

Page number
Date, written as MM/DD/YY

Title of the experiment
Memory verse
Hypothesis, when appropriate.

Experimental details, data, drawings, observations.

Conclusion: What did you learn?

Further questions: What do you want to learn?

EXAMPLE   Page: 76
                 10/15/16

Magnets, what will stick?
Proverbs 18:24, A friend sticks closer than a brother.

Material	Hypothesis	Observation
Plastic cup	YES	NO
Nail	Yes	YES
Soccer ball	NO	NO
Penny	YES	NO
Door Hinge	YES	YES

Some metals will stick to a magnet. Why? What makes some metals stick?

POTENTIAL & KINETIC ENERGY

Define, compare, and contrast potential and kinetic energy.
Experiment with potential and kinetic energy using playground equipment.

MATERIALS

1. A ball that is easy to catch and throw

2. Playground swing

3. Slide

Hazards: As always, use caution on playground equipment.

ENERGY

Does your mother ever say, "You have too much energy!"

Can you show me energy? Encourage the students to show you their energy by moving.

There are actually two different kinds of energy. The first kind of energy is energy of motion, **kinetic energy**. The energy you just showed me is kinetic energy because you were really moving.

The other kind of energy is **potential energy**, which is stored energy. Or energy based upon position.

For instance: If you are sitting still on your bike at the top of a hill, you have potential energy (like possible energy). You are sitting still, but you have the potential, or possibility, to roll down the hill. When you begin to roll, the potential energy turns into kinetic energy because you are moving.

BIG IDEA

CONSIDER THESE EXAMPLES ALSO:

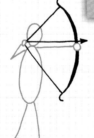

- Bow and arrow: When the bow is pulled back, it has potential energy. When the arrow is released, it has kinetic energy. (The potential energy is converted into kinetic energy.)

- A rock held high: When the rock is held up, it has potential energy. When the rock is dropped, it has kinetic energy. (The potential energy is converted into kinetic energy.)

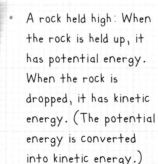

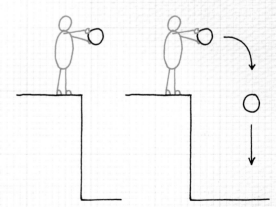

- Allow children to brainstorm more examples. Here are some hints: pulling back a rubber band, snow skiing down a hill, or water being poured out of a cup.

- (Note: there may be some confusion with chemical energy. This energy is stored in chemical bonds. It can be released to create motion or heat. Examples include burning gasoline to make a car move, burning wood to heat a house, or eating food to have energy to move.)

ENERGY

SLIDE:

ACTIVITY
1

1. Ask a child to sit at the top of the slide. What kind of energy does he or she have when sitting still at the top of the slide? (potential)

2. Then ask the child to slide down. What kind of energy does he or she have while sliding down? (kinetic)

3. Have the children take turns sliding. Saying "POTENTIAL ENERGY" while sitting at the top of the slide, and "KINETIC ENERGY" while sliding down.

At the top of the slide, the child only has potential energy. Then as he or she slides down, the potential energy is converted into kinetic energy.

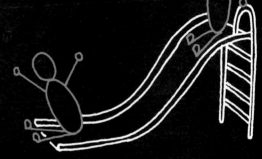

SWING:

1. Ask a child to sit in a swing. Pull the swing back and hold the chains, so that the child is waiting to swing forward. While holding the swing back, ask what kind of energy does the swing have right now, before it moves? (potential)

ACTIVITY
2

2. Then let the swing go so the child swings forward. What kind of energy does he have while swinging? (kinetic)

3. Have the children take turns swinging. Saying "POTENTIAL ENERGY" when the chains are pulled back and "KINETIC ENERGY" while the swing is in motion.

4. If the children really understand this concept, explain that when the swing is at the apex, it has potential energy. It stops for just a moment before turning around. Then that potential energy is converted to kinetic energy as the swing descends.

(A) is the pause at the apex of the swing, when all of the energy is potential. (B) is the lowest point of the swing, when all of the energy is kinetic. On the path of the swing in between point (A) and (B), the energy is partially kinetic and partially potential.

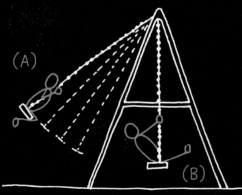
(A)
(B)

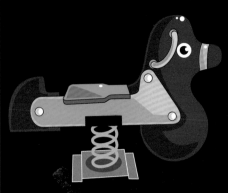

SPRING RIDER:

ACTIVITY
3

1. Ask a child to sit on a spring rider. Pull the spring rider back, so the spring is under tension, ready to pull the child forward. While holding the spring rider back, ask what kind of energy is this? (potential)

2. Then release the spring rider so that it moves forward. What kind of energy is this? (kinetic)

3. Have the children take turns riding. Saying "POTENTIAL ENERGY" when the spring is pulled back and "KINETIC ENERGY" while the spring rider is in motion.

4. If the children really understand this concept, explain that when the spring has the ability to store energy. When it reaches its maximum, it has potential energy. It stops for just a moment before turning around. Then that potential energy is converted to kinetic energy as the spring recoils.

ACTIVITY
4

ENERGY FROM GOD

Colossians 1:19 tells us that, "To this end I strenuously contend with all the energy Christ so powerfully works in me."

God is the source of our energy. This energy gives us the ability to get out of bed in the morning, to run, and to play. The energy God provides for us is divine and beyond anything science can describe. God's energy is like an endless well of potential energy, ready to flow powerfully through us. Mark 16:15 tells us to, "Go into all the world and preach the gospel to all creation." We are commanded to "go". Energy of motion is kinetic energy. We are to take God's divine potential energy and use it as kinetic energy in this world. That powerful potential energy from God will work in YOU, so you have the kinetic energy to go and obey His commands. This is wonderful news. We cannot even draw one breath without the Lord, we cannot do anything without His energy. We can rely on Him to work "so powerfully" in us, spreading the good news of Jesus to the whole world.

1. Form a hypothesis: If a ball is tossed up in the air, will it come down?

   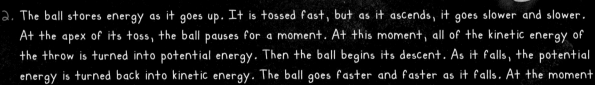

   1. Test the hypothesis by gently tossing the ball straight up.

   2. The ball stores energy as it goes up. It is tossed fast, but as it ascends, it goes slower and slower. At the apex of its toss, the ball pauses for a moment. At this moment, all of the kinetic energy of the throw is turned into potential energy. Then the ball begins its descent. As it falls, the potential energy is turned back into kinetic energy. The ball goes faster and faster as it falls. At the moment the ball is caught, it is going the same speed as it was going at the moment it was thrown.

   3. Every time you toss a ball, remember that God's divine potential energy works in you to give you kinetic energy to do His will. Practice the memory verse as you toss the ball back and forth.

2. The further an object is from the SOURCE of energy, the less energy it receives from that source. We must remember this when we think and pray. The closer we are to God's divine energy, the more alive we will be. What are some things you can do to stay close to God's divine energy?

- There are simple examples of kinetic and potential energy all around. Here are a few to look for as you go through life:

    o A delivery man unloading a truck down a ramp.

    o Rolling a ball down a sloped driveway.

    o Passing a football.

    o Jumping on a trampoline.

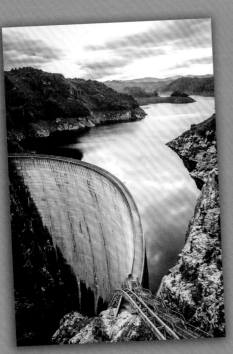

- Make two labels to place on the slide "Potential Energy" at the top where the children sit, and "Kinetic Energy →" pointing down the slide.

- Use a marker to write Colossians 1:19-20 on a playground ball. Let it be a reminder of God's energy every time the students play with it.

- Go to a dam with your child. Look at the lake on one side, and the river flowing on the other side. The water in the lake has potential energy while the river has kinetic energy. What would happen if the dam broke? How can people use the energy stored behind the dam? Study hydroelectric power.

- The law of conservation of energy states that energy cannot be created or destroyed, only change form. How is this true for the kinetic and potential energy of the playground equipment? Can you create your own demonstration for the law of conservation of energy?

o Can you relate this law of science to Colossians 1:20? However, remember that God the Creator is not constrained by the laws of science.

ENERGY

SIMPLE MACHINES
IN A PLAYGROUND

Understand the six simple machines (as defined by Renaissance scientists), identify any simple machines found in a playground.

MATERIALS

1. A well-equipped playground (Not all six simple machines may be present at any one playground; identify those that are available.)
2. One plastic jar for each child
3. Stickers
4. Ribbon
5. Glue
6. Other small decorations for the jar
7. Slips of paper,
8. Writing utensils

What do you think of when you hear the word "machine"? (car, tractor, power tools, bulldozer, vacuum cleaner, etc.) Wow! Those machines are so complicated. There are machines all around us that are much more simple. You use them all of the time and never even realize it. They help you be stronger or go faster by increasing your force, or they sometimes just change the direction of your force. The name of these machines is so easy to remember; they are called "simple machines." Today we are going to look for six simple machines.

BIG IDEA

Lever	Pulley	Wheel and axle	Inclined plane	Wedge	Screw

 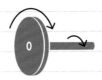 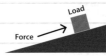

1. **Lever** – helps people do work by pivoting an object on a fulcrum.
2. **Pulley** – helps people pull heavy loads up or across.
3. **Wheel and axle** – helps people move or lift loads.
4. **Inclined plane** – a ramp that helps people move heavy loads up and down.
5. **Wedge** – helps people spread or cut some things apart.
6. **Screw** – help people hold thing together or move heavy loads up and down.

SIMPLE MACHINES

SIMPLE MACHINE HUNT:

CAN YOU FIND ANY OF THESE ON THE PLAYGROUND?

Begin by asking the students to find an inclined plane. If they have trouble, give hints to narrow their search. Then proceed to search for some of the other simple machines on the following list. This list is not comprehensive; you may find many more simple machines than are listed here. (Note: Many simple machines fall into more than one category. For example, while a door on hinges functions primarily as a lever, almost all types of hinges feature a wheel and axel as well.)

Lever	Wheel & axle	Pulley	Inclined plane	Wedge	Screw
• Seesaw • Door on hinges • Toilet flush handle	• Door knob • Wagon • Bike • Wheel chair • Toy car	• Flag pole • Crane	• Slide • Sloping hill • Water slide • Wheel chair ramp	• Zipper • Lawn mower blade • Cutting tool • Nail in wood	• Bolt or screw • Spiral staircase • Spiral slide

GOD'S BLESSING JAR:

1. Looking for simple machines on the playground is like a treasure hunt. If we look hard enough, we can find simple machines all around us. If we follow Jesus, we are living a real-life treasure hunt. But the great news is that the treasure is already ours! From the moment you put your trust in Christ, you are blessed.

> Ephesians 1:3 says, "Praise be to the God and Father of our Lord Jesus Christ, who has blessed us in the heavenly realms with every spiritual blessing in Christ."

Through all of eternity we will discover the riches of God's mercy. We are spiritually wealthy beyond measure. It is important for us to learn to open our eyes and hearts to see the riches He has lavished upon us.

2. Give each child a jar. Allow them to decorate and personalize their jar. Make sure Ephesians 1:3 is written on each child's jar.

3. When the jars are complete, give each child a few slips of paper. Instruct them to draw or write some blessings in their lives. Then give them a few more slips of paper. Ask them to write more blessings. Repeat this process until they are having trouble thinking of blessings. This is where the real treasure hunting begins. Some blessings are easy to find, others require more thought.

4. Every day for the next year, write a blessing and drop it in the jar. Try not to write the same blessing twice.

5. At a family gathering in the next year, open the jars and read the blessings out loud. This is a splendid reminder of God's faithfulness, in good times and in bad.

- Any time you notice a simple machine, repeat Ephesians 1:3. Simple machines are hidden all around us. It is easy to walk right by them without noticing. Just as God's blessings are all around us, and we so often fail to notice.

- Can you find any of these at home?

Lever	Wheel & axle	Pulley	Inclined plane	Wedge	Screw
• Claw of a hammer • Bottle opener • Scissors • Stapler • Curling iron • Car door handle • Fishing pole	• Car tire and axle • Fertilizer cart • Roller skates • Bike • Stroller	• Clothes line • Mini blinds • Exercise equipment	• 4 wheeler ramps • Moving ramp • Wheel chair ramp	• Ax for cutting wood • Hand held pencil sharpener blade • Knife	• Screw top bottle or jar • A loose screw

- Combining simple machines often makes work easier. If two or more simple machines are put together, they are called a compound machine. For example, cranes use levers, wheels and axles, and many pulleys to lift heavy objects.

- Study Archimedes of Syracus, a Greek scientist who did much of the early research regarding simple machines.

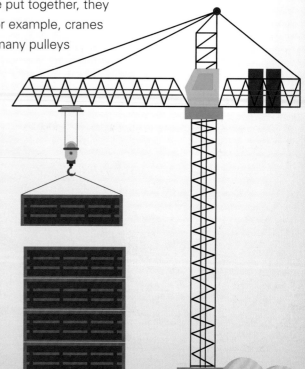

SIMPLE MACHINES

Experiment 3:

MECHANICAL ADVANTAGE OF A LEVER

Learn the definition of mechanical advantage, lever, fulcrum, load end, and effort end. Explore how a lever is a helpful tool. Determine that placing the fulcrum closer to the load end creates a greater mechanical advantage.

BIG IDEA

God made His children with very inventive minds.

People love to solve problems and make hard jobs easier. Imagine when God first created people, and they wanted to build houses. What did they have to invent? (hammer, nails, boards, roof, etc.) They had to create tools. **Tools are simple machines that give people a mechanical advantage.** Say those words a few times together, "mechanical advantage." Mechanical advantage is when a person is made stronger by using a tool. What are some tools you or your parents use? (washing machine, drill, hedge clippers, etc.) A simple machine is an uncomplicated tool. Do you remember the six basic simple machines? Wheel and axel, inclined plane, screw, pulley, wedge, and lever.

HEAVY LIFTING:

ACTIVITY 1

1. Today we are going to explore how to use a simple machine called a **lever** to make jobs easier.

2. Place the book on table. Ask your child to lift the book. Is it heavy?

3. Position the end of the paint stick well under the edge of the book. This is the **load** end of the lever.

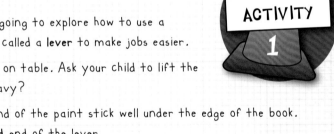

Load   Effort

Load Arm   Fulcrum   Effort Arm

ADV. OF A LEVER

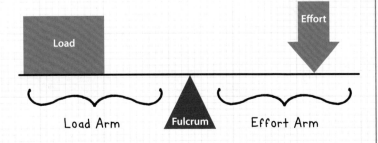

MATERIALS

1. Sturdy ruler or paint stick

2. A 1 inch binder clip (with handles removed or folded flat together) or other prism shape of approximately 1 inch height

3. Something rather heavy (like a text book or brick)

4. Two small cups

5. Tape,

6. About 50 pennies

7. A playground see saw. If a see-saw is not available, have the children balance their ruler or paint stick on their finger for Activity 3

4. Move the binder clip under the stick, near the opposite end. The binder clip is the fulcrum.

5. Ask your child to try to use the lever, press on the effort end, to lift the book off the table. Is it possible? (The book may not balance perfectly on the paint stick. This is not a problem as the student will still be able to feel the difference in effort.)

6. Move the binder clip/fulcrum under the paint stick, near the center.

7. Ask your child to press on the effort end again. Is it easier?

8. Form a hypothesis: how can we make lifting the book even easier?

9. Move the binder clip/fulcrum even closer to the book. Is it easier to lift?

10. What have you learned about heavy lifting with a lever? Levers can make lifting easier, especially when the fulcrum is closer to the load end/heavy object. Levers give people a mechanical advantage.

BALANCING PENNY ACT:

1. Tape a cup to each end of the paint stick. Write "load" on one cup and "effort" on the other cup.

2. Place the binder clip/fulcrum about 1/3 of the distance from the effort end.

3. Place five pennies in the load end cup.

4. Form a hypothesis: How many pennies will it take to lift the five pennies?

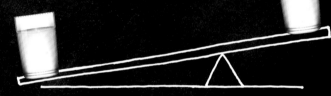

5. Experiment: Add pennies, one at a time, to the effort end until the load end lifts up.

6. Form a hypothesis: Which way should the fulcrum be moved so that it takes LESS pennies on the effort end to lift the five penny load? In other words, which way should the fulcrum be moved for a greater mechanical advantage?

7. Experiment: Move the fulcrum about one inch in the direction your child decides. Keeping five pennies in the load end, add one penny at a time to the effort end until the load is lifted. Was the hypothesis correct?

8. Form a hypothesis: Which way should the fulcrum be moved so to that it takes MORE pennies on the effort end to lift the five penny load? In other words, which way should the fulcrum be moved for a lesser mechanical advantage?

9. Experiment: Move the fulcrum about one inch in the direction your child decides. Keeping five pennies in the load end, add one penny at a time to the effort end until the load is lifted. Was the hypothesis correct?

10. Allow your child freedom to experiment with more and less pennies on the load end. Allow your child to move the fulcrum freely.

ADV. OF A LEVER

EXPERIMENT 3: MECHANICAL ADVANTAGE OF A LEVER

SEESAW OPPOSITES:

ACTIVITY
3

1. Allow children to seesaw with one child on each end, experimenting with partners of greater or lesser weight. Identify the fulcrum, lever, load, and effort. Note that the child going up is on the load end and the child going down is on the effort end. When attention spans wane, continue the lesson.

2. As you have learned, when one side of a lever goes up, the other side goes down. They are opposites.

3. Sometimes it is not easy to obey God's commands. Sometimes we are tempted to do the opposite of what we know is righteous.

    a. Has your mom ever asked you to pick up your toys? Have you ever obeyed her? Have you ever disobeyed her?

    b. Has your friend ever asked you to share? Have you ever shared your toy with love? Have you ever not shared your toy to keep it to yourself?

4. Group the children into pairs such that the pair of children have similar weight and vocabulary skills. Have two children sit on opposite ends of the seesaw. A seesaw is an example of a simple lever. Read a negative term from the list on the left. While they are seesawing, ask the children to think of the opposite positive terms, they can brain storm several synonyms.

Negative	Opposite positive
Angry	Loving, forgiving, peaceful, quiet, relaxed, calm, warm, nice.
Unbelieving	Trusting, faithful, hopeful.
Dishonest	Truthful, honest, correct, faithful, reliable.
Ungrateful	Thankful, appreciative, content.
Greedy	Generous, giving, kind, big-hearted.
Miserable	Joyful, happy, pleased, glad, elated, thrilled.
Lazy	Hard working, helpful, cooperative, caring, supportive.
Proud	Humble, modest, respectful, gentle, caring.
Irritable	Patient, uncomplaining, relaxed, agreeable
Cowardly	Courageous, bold, brave, daring.

Phillipians 4:8 says "Finally, brothers and sisters, whatever is true, whatever is noble, whatever is right, whatever is pure, whatever is lovely, whatever is admirable—*if anything is excellent or praiseworthy—think about such things.*

5. God commands us to focus on anything that is "excellent or praiseworthy" in every situation. This can be difficult and take practice. Read over the list again phrased as comparison questions. For example, "does God want us to be angry or forgiving?"

- Ask your child to find levers in his/her world: a pair of scissors, a wheel barrow, the handle of a sink (not a knob), the human jaw bone (mandible), the pedals of a car, door handles (not door knobs), seesaw, the human arm and elbow, toilet flusher, stapler, salad tongs.

- When your child exhibits negative thinking, review Philippians 4:8.

READ THE STORY OF ESAU & JACOB FROM GENESIS 25:24-34

When the time came for [Rebekah] to give birth, there were twin boys in her womb. The first to come out was red, and his whole body was like a hairy garment; so they named him Esau. After this, his brother came out, with his hand grasping Esau's heel; so he was named Jacob. Isaac was sixty years old when Rebekah gave birth to them.

The boys grew up, and Esau became a skillful hunter, a man of the open country, while Jacob was content to stay at home among the tents. Isaac, who had a taste for wild game, loved Esau, but Rebekah loved Jacob.

Once when Jacob was cooking some stew, Esau came in from the open country, famished. He said to Jacob, "Quick, let me have some of that red stew! I'm famished!" (That is why he was also called Edom.)

Jacob replied, "First sell me your birthright."

Look, I am about to die," Esau said. "What good is the birthright to me?"

But Jacob said, "Swear to me first." So he swore an oath to him, selling his birthright to Jacob.

Then Jacob gave Esau some bread and some lentil stew. He ate and drank, and then got up and left.

So Esau despised his birthright.

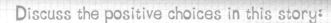

Discuss the positive choices in this story:

- Esau was a skillful hunter
- Jacob was content to stay at home
- Jacob wanted the birthright

Discuss the negative choices in this story:

- Isaac loved Esau more while Rebekah loved Jacob more
- Esau was impatient for food.
- Esau exaggerated the truth
- Jacob used Esau's hunger to manipulate him
- Esau did not value his birthright; he despised it
- Esau ate and left without saying thank you.

ADVANTAGE OF A LEVER

- Choose four children to play the parts of Rebekah, Isaac, Esau, and Jacob. Read the story again while the children act out their parts. Props may be used to enhance the performance.

- Discuss the following: Esau wanted immediate satisfaction. He sold something priceless for a bowl of soup. This sounds so ridiculous to us. How could anyone trade everything for something so inferior? What is the birthright of believers? To inherit the kingdom of God by accepting Christ. This is so precious, we must never treat it cheaply. Value your birthright, treasure it every day, never trade something temporary for what God is giving you for eternity.

APPLY IT
CONTINUED...

GO BEYOND

Study the center of gravity of a broom.

- Ask your child to hold a broom, balanced on one finger from each hand. Begin by holding your fingers a couple of feet apart, then slowly slide your fingers closer together. The broom will just balance when your two fingers meet at the center of gravity. It may take several tries to find the center of gravity. Why is the center of gravity of the broom not in the center of the broom handle?

Drive a nail about a half inch into a board.

[PLEASE USE ADULT SUPERVISION.]

- Ask your child to try to pull the nail out with his hand. Then allow him to use the claw of a hammer to pull the nail. It will be much easier. Why is it easier to pull the nail with a hammer? The hammer is a lever; where it touches the board is a fulcrum.

  o Pulling the nail out can be made even easier by using a small wooden block under the head of the hammer to create a fulcrum closer to the head of the nail.

- Study, find examples of, and build the three different types of levers.

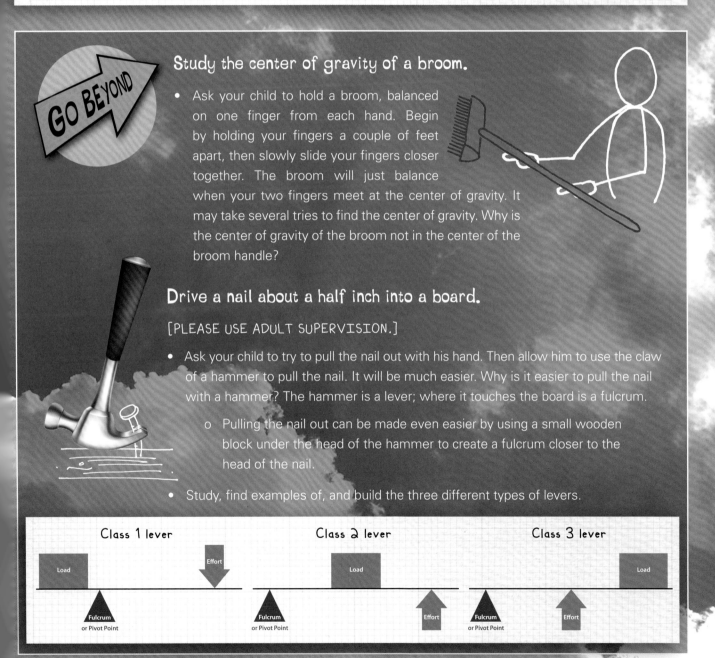

Class 1 lever	Class 2 lever	Class 3 lever
Load — Effort — Fulcrum or Pivot Point	Load — Fulcrum or Pivot Point — Effort	Load — Fulcrum or Pivot Point — Effort

FIXED PULLEY:
CHANGING THE DIRECTION OF FORCE

Understand how a pulley creates a change in direction of force.
Build a simple fixed pulley.

MATERIALS

1. Wire coat hanger
2. Empty thread or ribbon spool
3. Two paper or plastic cups
4. About 6 feet of string
5. About 30 pennies
6. Two sheets of paper
7. Writing utensils
8. Two carabineers or sturdy napkin rings
9. About 20 feet of lightweight rope

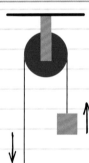

Have you ever had to lift anything heavy?

What if you could use a simple machine to lift the heavy object?

One tool people use to lift or move heavy objects is a pulley. This is a simple wheel with a groove around it, on an axle. It supports a cable or rope around the wheel.

BIG IDEA

ACTIVITY 1

BUILD A SIMPLE FIXED PULLEY:

1. Untwist the top of the coat hanger. Thread it through the empty spool.
2. Re-twist the top of the coat hanger and hang it so that it is more than three feet off the floor and has plenty of space around it.
3. Punch holes just under the rims of the cups, and tie them to each end of the six foot string.
4. Hang the string over the spool so the cups can hold the pennies.
5. Adjust the string so that one of the cups is hanging above the floor and the other cup is resting on the floor.
6. Place 10 pennies in the cup that is touching the floor.
7. One at a time, add pennies to the other cup. How many pennies does it take to lift up the cup with 10 pennies?
8. **Pulleys can change the direction of force.** In this system, the pennies in the top cup exert a *down*ward force. The direction of this force is changed by the pulley to lift the other pennies *upward*.

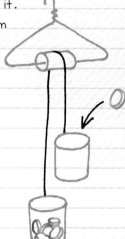

FIXED PULLEY

SAUL'S LIFE CHANGES DIRECTION:

1. Read Acts 9:1-22:

Saul was still breathing out murderous threats against the Lord's disciples. He went to the high priest and asked him for letters to the synagogues in Damascus, so that if he found any there who belonged to the Way, whether men or women, he might take them as prisoners to Jerusalem. As he neared Damascus on his journey, suddenly a light from heaven flashed around him. He fell to the ground and heard a voice say to him, "Saul, Saul, why do you persecute me?"

"Who are you, Lord?" Saul asked.

"I am Jesus, whom you are persecuting," he replied. "Now get up and go into the city, and you will be told what you must do."

The men traveling with Saul stood there speechless; they heard the sound but did not see anyone. Saul got up from the ground, but when he opened his eyes he could see nothing. So they led him by the hand into Damascus. For three days he was blind, and did not eat or drink anything.

In Damascus there was a disciple named Ananias. The Lord called to him in a vision, "Ananias!"

"Yes, Lord," he answered.

The Lord told him, "Go to the house of Judas on Straight Street and ask for a man from Tarsus named Saul, for he is praying. In a vision he has seen a man named Ananias come and place his hands on him to restore his sight."

"Lord," Ananias answered, "I have heard many reports about this man and all the harm he has done to your holy people in Jerusalem. And he has come here with authority from the chief priests to arrest all who call on your name."

But the Lord said to Ananias, "Go! This man is my chosen instrument to proclaim my name to the Gentiles and their kings and to the people of Israel. I will show him how much he must suffer for my name."

Then Ananias went to the house and entered it. Placing his hands on Saul, he said, "Brother Saul, the Lord – Jesus, who appeared to you on the road as you were coming here – has sent me so that you may see again and be filled with the Holy Spirit." Immediately, something like scales fell from Saul's eyes, and he could see again. He got up and was baptized, and after taking some food, he regained his strength.

Saul spent several days with the disciples in Damascus.

Acts 9:20 At once [Saul] began to preach in the synagogues that Jesus is the Son of God.

All those who heard him were astonished and asked, "Isn't he the man who raised havoc in Jerusalem among those who call on this name? And hasn't he come here to take them as prisoners to the chief priests? Yet Saul grew more and more powerful and baffled the Jews living in Damascus by proving that Jesus is the Messiah.

FIXED PULLEY

2. On one sheet of paper draw an arrow going down. On the other sheet of paper draw an arrow going up. Explain that Saul's life was going "down" fast before he knew Jesus. And after he knew Jesus, his life began to go "up." Like a pulley can change the direction of force, so Jesus can change the direction of a person's life.

3. Re-read the story. This time, ask children to point out characteristics of Saul's "down" life and Saul's "up" life. Have the children take turns writing the characteristics on the appropriate sheet. Younger children may prefer to draw them.

   a. For example:

      i. "Down" – breathing out murderous threats, putting believers in prison, persecuted the Lord, did harm to holy people, raised havoc in Jerusalem.

      ii. "Up" – called Jesus "Lord", chosen instrument to reach Gentiles, Kings, and people of Israel, Ananias called him Brother Saul, filled with the Holy Spirit, scales fell from Saul's eyes, he was Baptized, began to preach that Jesus is the Son of God, proved that Jesus is the Messiah.

4. Write Acts 9:20 boldly on the "Up" sheet.

5. Committing your life to Jesus will certainly change the direction of your life.

   a. Jesus changes your way of thinking. Sin weighs you down in this life, but with Jesus' forgiveness, that weight is lifted. He gives you a new heart and makes you a new creation. 1 John 1:9, Psalm 32.

   b. Jesus changes your future. Because of sin, we are all separated from God and on a path to hell. When you invite Jesus to be your savior, your destination changes! Because of Jesus, you will be going to heaven, the place he has prepared for those who love him. Matthew 25:46, 1 Corinthians 6:10-11, Isaiah 59:2, Romans 6:23.

   c. Jesus changes your path in this life. He will be with you for every moment from the time you accept him. He will guide you to become more like him. And he will never give up on you! 1 Thessalonians 5:23-24, Joshua 1:9, Matthew 28:20, Romans 8:28.

MOVABLE PULLEY TUG-OF-WAR:

ACTIVITY
3

1. Divide children into pairs ("child A" and "child B") of similar learning ability and strength.

2. Using 2 carabineers and 20 feet of rope:
   a. Tie one end of the string to one carabineer with a good knot.
   b. Thread the string through the second carabineer.

FIXED PULLEY

ACTIVITY 3 CONTINUED...

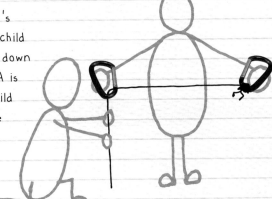

c. Have child A hold the two carabineers at arm's length apart. While child B faces child A, ask child B to pull the loose end of the string straight down from the second carabineer. Such that child A is trying to hold the carabineers apart while child B is pulling the string down to try to pull the carabineers together.

    i. Who succeeds? Was it difficult or easy?

d. Ask the children to trade places and try again.

3. Next, thread the string in and out of the carabineers three times.

    a. Form a hypothesis: Will it be easier or harder to pull the rings together?

    b. Repeat steps 2c and 2d.

4. Last, thread the string in and out of the carabineers two MORE times.

    a. Form a hypothesis: Will it be easier or harder to pull the rings together?

    b. Repeat steps 2c and 2d.

5. Pulleys can change the direction of force and decrease the required force. In this system, they do both. The pulleys change the direction of force; when one child pulls down, the rings move together. The pulleys also decrease the amount of force required to pull the rings together; the same amount of work is exerted over the longer distance of the rope.

APPLY IT

- How are shoe laces threaded through a shoe like a pulley? Can you pull your shoe tight without the laces?

- From a safe distance, observe a construction site. Look for pulleys on heavy equipment. Watch how the workers use the cranes to lift heavy beams. The cranes pull the cable down to lift the heavy object up.

- Look for pulleys on cable cars, clothes lines, ski lifts, flag poles, etc.

- Read the story of the stoning of Stephen in Acts 7. How does this contrast to Philippians 1:6?

Study the 3 missionary journeys of Paul.

Did God change the direction of his life?

- Read *Pull, Lift, and Lower: A Book about Pulleys* by Michael Dahl
- Study how archaeologists think the Egyptian pyramids were built.
- Build a pulley system for your child's bunk beds or tree house. Relatively inexpensive metal or plastic pulleys can be obtained from a hardware store.
- Many exercise machines contain pulley systems. With adult supervision, examine a weight-lifting machine, experiment with the weights and pulleys. Do the pulleys create a mechanical advantage? Why are there pulleys on the weight lifting machine?
   o Note a system with movable pulleys that can change the direction of force and/or decrease the amount of force required to lift an object.

GO BEYOND

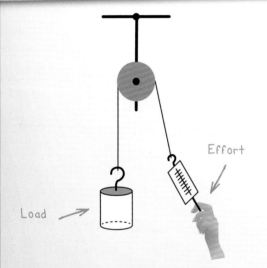

Effort

Load

How Fixed and Movable Pulleys Can Decrease Effort:

Note: Newtons (International system) and pounds (English system) are common units of force. One pound of force is equal to 4.45 newtons of force.

Imagine a heavy rock (load) with a mass of 100 newtons hooked to one pulley. In order for the rock to be lifted up, 100 newtons of downward force (effort) are needed. If you pull in 1 meter of rope, the rock will raise 1 meter. You have no mechanical advantage, just a change in direction of force.

The more wheels there are in a pulley system, the less effort is needed to lift the load. In order to find the mechanical advantage of a pulley system, count the ropes, but do not count the effort rope if it pulls in the opposite direction as the movement of the load (if you pull down to raise the load up, do not count the effort rope).

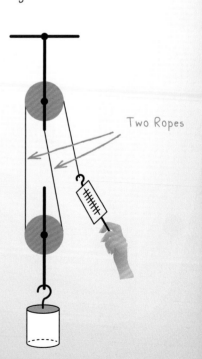

Two Ropes

Suppose there are two wheels in the pulley system to lift the 100 newton rock, one fixed pulley at the top and one movable pulley on the load. It will only take 50 newtons of force to lift the rock. Mechanical advantage is how much the pulley multiplies force. The more pulleys, the greater the mechanical advantage. The greater the mechanical advantage, the less force you have to apply to do the work. But the lesser force you apply must be over a longer distance of rope. In the system described here, in order to raise the rock 1 meter, you must pull in 2 meters of rope.

FIXED PULLEY

What force would be needed to lift the 100 Newton rock if there are four pulleys in the system? 25 newtons. And you would pull in four times as much rope. What an amazing mechanical advantage! Note: many pulleys are made with several wheels in a single housing. Each wheel counts as a pulley.

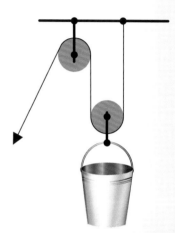

One pulley

Two pulley

Example: You have one pulley, one bucket, and one rope. The pulley is mounted above a well. If this pulley system is used to lower and raise the bucket down into the well, the pulley only changes the direction so it takes 60 lb of effort to lift the 60 lb of water.

BUT what if you attached one end of the rope to the well house, then threaded the rope through a movable pulley on the bucket, and then threaded the remaining end of the rope through a fixed pulley? How much effort would it take to pull up the 60 lb bucket? Count the ropes. But do not count the effort rope since it pulls in the opposite direction as the motion of the load. It would only take 30 lb of effort...of course you would pull in twice as much rope.

If the effort is in the same direction as the movement of the load, the pulley system gives a mechanical advantage, but does not change the direction of force.

For example, consider if you attached one end of the rope to the well house, then through a movable pulley on the bucket, through a fixed pulley, and then through a second movable pulley on the bucket. How much effort would it take to pull up the 60 lb bucket? Count the ropes. This time, DO count the effort rope since it pulls in the SAME direction as the motion of the load (you pull up to move the load up). It would only take 15 lb of effort...of course you would pull in four times as much rope.

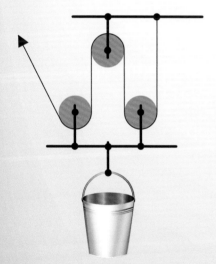

Consider the following pulley systems. How much effort would it take to lift the 60 lb load?

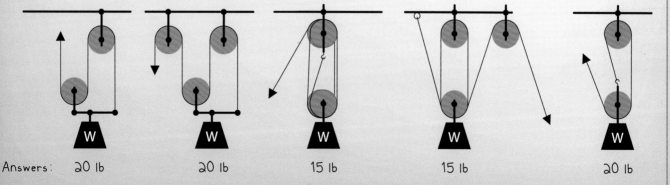

Answers: 20 lb   20 lb   15 lb   15 lb   20 lb

ANGULAR MOMENTUM AND CENTRIPETAL MOTION:

To understand the meaning of angular momentum in terms of a rotating object. Demonstrate centripetal motion and Newton's First law of motion.

MATERIALS

1. A playground swing with long chains

2. A small, sturdy bucket with a secure handle

3. Water

4. One strip of paper for each child plus a few extra strips (1 inch wide, 11 inches long)

4. Tape

5. Writing utensils

Genesis 1:1 tells us that "In the beginning, **God** created the heavens and the earth."

BIG IDEA

God set everything in motion when He created the universe. One of the kinds of motion we see is spinning motion. Can you think of anything that spins or moves in a circle? (ballerina, ice skater, earth on its axis, spinning basketball, etc). Today, we are going to experiment with **angular momentum** and **centripetal motion.**

- Angular momentum is how an object spins on its axis. Think of a top spinning in place.

- Centripetal motion is circular motion. Think of a satellite orbiting the earth or a stone tied to a string being swung in a circle.

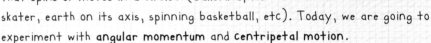

SWING & ANGULAR MOMENTUM:

Hazards: make sure the swing is sturdy. Instruct children to hold on tight. Use a baby swing if child is too young to hold on properly. The children will be dizzy after experiencing angular momentum.

1. Ask a child to sit in the playground swing.

2. While standing stationary, spin the child in the swing seat in order to wind the chains up, up, up (at least 5 or 8 turns).

3. Form a hypothesis: What will happen when the swing is released?

4. Test the hypothesis. Release the swing and let the child spin. Say, "ANGULAR MOMENTUM" as the swing spins.

5. Let the children take turns, saying "ANGULAR MOMENTUM" every time the swing spins.

CENTRIPETAL MOTION

ACTIVITY 1

INERTIA:

CENTRIPETAL MOTION

ACTIVITY 2

1. This is the same as Activity 1, except have the child extend his legs and torso out before the swing is released.

2. Release the swing. Then ask him or her to tuck his or her arms and legs in. (This decreases the child's inertia and increases his or her rate of rotation).

3. What happened to the speed of the spin?

4. Next, wind the chains up again. Form a hypothesis: What will happen to the speed of the spin if the child begins the spin with arms and legs tucked in, then extends his or her body half way through the spin? (This increases the child's inertia and decreases his or her rate of rotation).

CENTRIPETAL MOTION

SWINGING A BUCKET FULL OF WATER: BEST IF DONE OUTSIDE

ACTIVITY 3

1. Fill the bucket about half way with water.

2. Form a hypothesis: Can the bucket be turned upside down without the water spilling?

3. Let the children test their hypothesis.

4. Ask the children to stand back for safety.

5. Then the teacher demonstrates that the bucket can be quickly swung in a vertical circle without spilling the water.

6. Be careful not to swing the bucket too slowly.

Is the water in the bucket defying gravity? Gravity is still pulling down on the water, even when it is above your head. According to Newton's first law of motion, objects in motion tend to remain in motion unless acted upon by an outside force. This is known as inertia. The water's inertia is pulling it in a straight path (imagine if you suddenly released the handle of the spinning bucket). However, gravity is pulling the water down toward the earth. While the water is falling, the bucket is falling with it. By swinging the bucket, you provide the force to overcome the force of gravity. This is centripetal force. It keeps the bucket and water moving around a circular path as directed by your arm (the radius). It pulls the bucket and water toward the center of the circle and keeps them from following the straight path of inertia. Centripetal motion is simply movement in this circular path. (Note to teachers: The force that pushes the water toward the outside of the circle, keeping it in the bucket, is centrifugal force. The force that pulls the bucket toward the center of the circle is centripetal force).

GOD'S LOVE MÖBIUS CIRCLE

Depending on the dexterity of the students, this can be done as a demonstration or as a student activity.

1. Circle 1: Use one strip of paper to create a simple circle. Tape it in place.

2. Circle 2: Use another strip of paper to create a second loop, but put a full twist (360 degrees) in one end before taping it.

3. Circle 3: Use a third strip of paper to create a Möbius loop by simply putting a half twist (180 degrees) in one end before taping it.

4. Ask children to examine the three circles of paper. How many sides do they have?

5. Hold up circle 1. This circle is like how God created Adam and Eve in the beginning. They were in complete union with Him. However, when they sinned, it caused separation from God. Use scissors to cut a straight line down the center of the circle to create two separate circles. This is what sin does, it separates us completely from God.

6. Hold up circle 2. But God still loved His children so much, that he sent Jesus to die for our sins. We are forgiven of the sin that separated us from God. Use scissors to cut a straight line down the center of circle 2. Hold up two linked circles. Now, nothing can separate us from God!

7. Hold up circle 3. God promises to love us, unconditionally. His love brings blessings to us, it does not matter how unlovable we may be.

In Hebrews **13:5** , the **Lord** says, "Never will I leave you; Never will I forsake you."

Use scissors to cut a straight line down the center of circle 3. Hold up the single continuous circle. God's love is eternal and unfailing! Our Lord never changes.

8. Ask children to write Hebrews 13:5 on a strip of paper. Then tape it to create a Möbius loop.

CENTRIPETAL MOTION

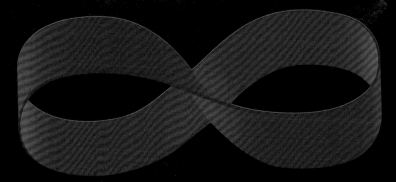

- Look for angular momentum as you go through your day: pinwheel, ice skater, spiraling football.

- Look for examples of centripetal motion as you go through your day. Like a car tire or bike tire spinning, a merry-go-round, Ferris wheel.

APPLY IT

Further Bible Study:

- Separation from God: Genesis 3, Isaiah 59:2, Romans 3:23, Romans 6:23

- Jesus' sacrifice: Isaiah 53:5, Romans 4:25, 1 Peter 3:18

- God's love: Psalm 102:12, John 3:16, Romans 8:37-39, Ephesians 2:4-5, Romans 5:8

- Study the two scientists who independently discovered the Möbius loop, August Ferdinand Möbius and Johann Benedict Listing.

GO BEYOND

Angular Momentum:

- Watch a figure skater spin faster when her arms and legs are tucked in, then slower when she extends her arms and legs. This is a wonderful demonstration of conservation of angular momentum. She reduces her inertia by pulling in her arms, thus increasing her rate of rotation.

Centripetal Motion:

- Let your child try to swing the water around in the bucket. Alternatively, a tennis ball on a string demonstrates centripetal motion quite well.

- Find a playground merry-go-round. Spin it and let your child feel the circular motion and centrifugal force pushing them toward the outside edge of the circle.

  o Place a pebble on the outer edge of the still merry go round, begin spinning the merry go round. Slowly at first, then speed up until the pebble spins off. Ask, why did the pebble spin off? The centrifugal force overcame the friction and gravity that held the pebble to the merry go round.

  o Experiment with different size pebbles at various distances from the center. Allow your child to draw his own conclusions.

- Research the differences between centripetal force and centrifugal force.

CENTRIPETAL MOTION

Experiment 6:

BUOYANCY OF BOATS

Understand buoyancy. Experiment with water displacement and buoyancy using student-created boats.

MATERIALS

1. Clear plastic cups
2. Markers
3. 5-10 waterproof objects (some of which float and some of which sink)
4. Aluminum foil
5. Clay
6. Craft sticks
7. Scrap fabric
8. Toothpicks
9. Wax paper
10. Bowl or bucket of water
11. 50-100 pennies
12. Paper for each child
13. Pencils
14. Crayons

(Optional: glue, cotton balls, blue tissue paper).

Mark 4:35-41
Jesus Calms the Storm

That day when evening came, he said to his disciples, "Let us go over to the other side." Leaving the crowd behind, they took him along, just as he was, in the boat. There were also other boats with him. A furious squall came up, and the waves broke over the boat, so that it was nearly swamped. Jesus was in the stern, sleeping on a cushion. The disciples woke him and said to him, "Teacher, don't you care if we drown?"

He got up, rebuked the wind and said to the waves, "Quiet! Be still!" Then the wind died down and it was completely calm.

> **Mark 35:40, [Jesus] said to his disciples, "Why are you so afraid? Do you still have no faith?"**

They were terrified and asked each other, "Who is this? Even the wind and the waves obey him!"

Have you ever been on a boat? The story says that "the waves broke over the boat, so that it was nearly swamped." What were the disciples worried about? What would happen if the boat was swamped or filled with water? Would you have been worried if you were in a boat that was filling with water?

BIG IDEA

Does a metal boat float or sink on water?

Does a metal nail float on or sink in water?

How can it be that a boat floats, but a nail sinks?

WATER DISPLACEMENT:

1. Give each student a clear cup half full of water. Have them use a marker to indicate the water level.

2. Have each student choose an object to drop in the water.

3. Form a hypothesis: What will happen to the water level when the object is dropped into the water? Mark your prediction on the cup with a line and write an "h" beside it for "hypothesis."

4. When forming a hypothesis or discussing an outcome, encourage the students to consider mass, size, and density.

5. Test the hypothesis by dropping the object into the water. Did it float or sink? How much did the water level change? Was your hypothesis correct?

6. Advanced students can use a ruler to measure and record how much the water level rises.

7. Water displacement is simply the amount of water that the object moves out of the way.

   a. If the object sinks completely, then the volume of water displaced is equal to the volume of the sinking object.

   b. If the object floats, then the weight of the water displaced is equal to the weight of the floating object.

   c. This is the principle of buoyancy, which states that an object partially or totally submerged in water displaces water according to how much it weighs. The water pushes up against the object with a force equal to the weight of the water it displaces.

BOAT FLOAT:

1. Ask each student to build a small boat out of aluminum foil, clay, craft sticks, scrap fabric, toothpicks, wax paper, and other similar materials. They can build multiple boats if they desire. Younger students will probably do better with only aluminum foil and a model boat to duplicate.

2. Form a hypothesis: Will the boat float or sink?

3. Test the hypothesis in the bowl of water.

4. Ask students to make improvements until each student builds a boat that will float.

5. In order for a boat to be functional, it must have buoyancy. That means it displaces a weight of water equal to the weight of the boat.

BUOYANCY OF BOATS

SINK THE BOAT:

1. Ask students to add pennies to their boat one at a time until the boat sinks.

2. Which boat held the most pennies? Why?

3. Explain that a boat becomes waterlogged when it tips over, leaks, or large waves wash over it. The air space inside the boat causes the boat to displace a large of volume of water, thus causing it to be buoyant. When the boat becomes waterlogged, the air is replaced with water. Therefore, the air is no longer displacing the water, and the boat sinks. The volume of water displaced is equal to the volume of the sinking boat.

IN THE BOAT WITH JESUS:

Sometimes life is going along smoothly; everything is fine. Life is like a boat sailing quietly through a calm sea. Then a big storm blows up. Maybe someone we love gets very sick, maybe one of our parents loses his/her job, maybe a beloved pet dies. Have any of you ever encountered a storm?

Re read Mark 4:35-41. Where was Jesus? He was in the boat. If our faith is in Jesus, we will always face the storms with Him by our side. In life, we will face plenty of opposition and temptation. The storm may rock our boat, but it will never sink our boat. Nothing can take us away from Jesus; He is in the boat. We should never let the presence of a storm make us doubt the presence of Jesus.

In Mark 4:35-41, whose idea was it to cross the lake? It was Jesus's idea! He said, "Let us go over to the other side." The disciples were in the storm because they were following Jesus's instructions. Just because we find ourselves in a storm, it does not necessarily mean we have done something wrong. We do not always know why there are storms. Maybe God allows Satan to cause them, maybe God sends them to test us, maybe our world is just broken and full of storms, but God is so powerful, His purposes will always be served. Our faith will grow. God will use the storm to produce a good inside us.

Put your hope in the Lord, not in the boat. And do not be afraid.

1. Give each student a sheet of paper and crayons, pencils, and markers. Ask them to draw the boat (optional: glue craft sticks onto the paper to create a wooden boat).

2. Then, write the name Jesus in the boat. Then, draw a picture of themselves in the boat looking peaceful.

3. Then, draw the waves (optional: glue blue tissue paper down to create a turbulent ocean).

4. Last, draw the wind and the storm (optional: glue down cotton balls as clouds and slices of foil as lightening).

5. Have children write, "Why are you so afraid? Do you still have no faith?" on their pictures.

BUOYANCY OF BOATS

- Look for boats, ducks, floating leaves, floating bath toys, and other floating objects as you go through your week.
- While on dry land, ask your child to pick you up. It is impossible. Then, get into a swimming pool, lake, or hot tub. Ask your child to pick you up as you relax in the water. It is easy!

  o In the water, you displace the weight of water equal to your volume. Thus, the water pushes you up, helping the child lift you more easily than he or she can on land. This is buoyancy!

- Read and discuss James 1:2-8: "Consider it pure joy, my brothers and sisters, whenever you face trials of many kinds, because you know that the testing of your faith produces perseverance. Let perseverance finish its work so that you may be mature and complete, not lacking anything. If any of you lacks wisdom, you should ask God, who gives generously to all without finding fault, and it will be given to you. But when you ask, you must believe and not doubt, because the one who doubts is like a wave of the sea, blown and tossed by the wind. That person should not expect to receive anything from the Lord. Such a person is double-minded and unstable in all they do."

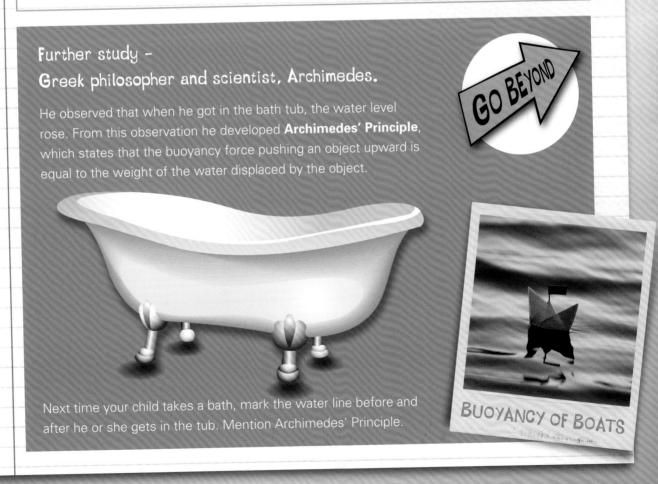

Further study – Greek philosopher and scientist, Archimedes.

He observed that when he got in the bath tub, the water level rose. From this observation he developed **Archimedes' Principle**, which states that the buoyancy force pushing an object upward is equal to the weight of the water displaced by the object.

GO BEYOND

Next time your child takes a bath, mark the water line before and after he or she gets in the tub. Mention Archimedes' Principle.

BUOYANCY OF BOATS

LAW OF CONSERVATION OF MATTER

Understand the word matter. Understand and memorize the law of conservation of matter. Examine several examples of the law of conservation of matter. Recognize examples of the law of conservation of matter beyond the classroom.

MATERIALS

1. An acorn and an oak tree (or any other large tree and one of its seeds)

2. An apple for snack (optional), two small cups

3. Baking soda

4. Vinegar

5. Gallon sized plastic baggie

6. Small kitchen scale

7. Small loaf of bread or baguette

When God created our world, he made all different kinds of things. He made trees, animals, water, rocks, etc.

BIG IDEA

What else did God create?

He gave us all of this to help us live, but only God can create things. The word for everything that God made is **matter**. What is matter? The table, the walls, the air, juice, etc.

Everything is matter.

Matter can change, but it cannot be created or destroyed; only God can do that. Repeat the law of conservation of matter several times:

Matter cannot be created or destroyed; only change form.

God made laws of nature to help the world function.

> Colossians 1:17 reminds us that "[the Lord] is before all things, and in him all things hold together."

CONSERVATION OF MATTER

THE GIANT OAK:

1. Let the students examine the tiny acorn. Ask, "What is this? This acorn may someday grow to be a huge tree." Then point out the tree. "How does this tiny acorn become an enormous tree?"

   a. Every oak tree was once an acorn. It fell from its "mother" tree. It was one of the few acorns that did not become food for birds, squirrels, or deer. It landed on that good spot of soil. First, a single root sprouted out of the shell. This root anchored the plant and began to absorb water. As the acorn absorbed more and more water, the shell cracked open, and a young seedling began to grow up toward the sun. Leaves emerged from the little oak and began to soak up sunlight. For years and years, the tree grew bigger.

2. Again, how exactly does this tiny acorn grow to become an enormous tree?

   a. When the roots absorb water, much of the water travels to the leaves and transpires (evaporates) off into the atmosphere. However, some of the water is incorporated into the structure of the plant. It changes from liquid water to be part of the leaf, root, stem, etc. The water changed form to become part of the plant.

   b. Carbon dioxide is made of two carbon atoms and one oxygen atom. Carbon dioxide, from the air, diffuses into the leaves of the oak. Using sunlight, the oak uses the carbon of the carbon dioxide to make sugars. The oxygen from the carbon dioxide diffuses back out into the air as a waste gas. The sugars are used by the plant to build roots, stems, bark, leaves, flowers, etc. So the carbon from the atmosphere changed form to become part of the plant.

   c. The soil provides nutrients like nitrogen, phosphorous, potassium, calcium, sulfur, and magnesium. These molecules travel into the plant with water it absorbs. They are key building blocks for the leaves, roots, trunk, etc. So the nutrients in the soil change form to become part of the plant.

      i. Fertilizers provide extra nitrogen, phosphorous, and potassium for the plants to use as it grows.

3. The acorn was only the beginning. The plant used soil, water, and carbon dioxide gas to grow. Matter was not created, it just changed form.

4. Consider an apple tree. Have you ever seen an apple seed? Review how an apple tree can grow so large.

   a. Enjoy eating the apple. You are eating sugars that were once gaseous carbon dioxide, water that was once in the dirt, and nutrients that came from the soil. The plant changed these into a delicious, juicy apple.

5. Matter cannot be created or destroyed; only change form.

6. Other examples:

   a. A fire burning a log: The log and oxygen from the atmosphere change into ash, smoke, and carbon dioxide.

   b. Metal rusting (oxidizing): Iron and oxygen combine to form rust.

   c. Baking a cake: Eggs, milk, flour, and sugar change into a solid cake.

   d. Ice cube melting into water: Solid water changes into liquid water.

   e. Consider how a child grows. Where does the food you eat and water you drink go?

   f. Ask the students to think of any other examples in which matter changes form.

CONSERVATION
OF MATTER

PRODUCTION OF A GAS:

1. Place about three tablespoons of vinegar in one small cup. Place about one tablespoon of baking soda in the other small cup.

2. Carefully set both cups upright in the gallon sized plastic baggie. Press as much air as possible out of the bag and seal it.

3. Using the kitchen scale, determine the total weight of the baggie, two cups, vinegar, and baking soda. Record this number for later comparison. This is the weight of the matter.

4. Form a hypothesis: Will the weight change if a chemical reaction takes place?

5. Without opening the bag, pour the vinegar into the baking soda cup.

6. Observe the gas produced during this chemical reaction. Do not open the bag.

7. When the reaction is complete, determine the weight. This includes the weight of the gas that was produced. How is it the same? All of the matter you placed in the baggie is still in the baggie. It has simply changed form.

8. Matter cannot be created or destroyed; only change form.

ACTIVITY
3

JESUS FEEDS 5000:

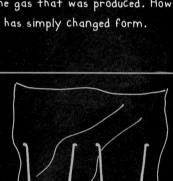

1. Since God created the law of conservation of matter, He can break it. After all, in the beginning, He created our entire universe from nothing. Listen to the story of Jesus feeding the Multitudes.

   a. **How** is this story a **miracle?**

   b. **How** does it break the **law of conservation of matter?**

Matthew 14: 13-21: When Jesus heard what had happened, he withdrew by boat privately to a solitary place. Hearing of this, the crowds followed him on foot from the towns. When Jesus landed and saw a large crowd, he had compassion on them and healed their sick.

   As evening approached, the disciples came to him and said, "This is a remote place, and it's already getting late. Send the crowds away, so they can go to the villages and buy themselves some food."

   Jesus replied, "They do not need to go away. You give them something to eat."

"We have here only five loaves of bread and two fish," they answered.

   "Bring them here to me," he said. And he directed the people to sit down on the grass. Taking the five loaves and the two fish and looking up to heaven, he gave thanks and broke the loaves. Then he gave them to the disciples, and the disciples gave them to the people. They all ate and were satisfied, and the disciples picked up twelve basketfuls of broken pieces that were left over. The number of those who ate was about five thousand men, besides women and children.

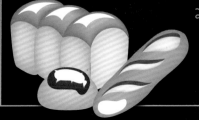

2. Pass a small loaf of homemade bread or a baguette around the room. Have the children tear off a piece for a snack as it passes by. There will probably not be enough to feed all of the children. Only God has the power to create or destroy matter. Have an extra snack on hand.

- When you water plants, repeat the law of conservation of matter. When you put gas in your car, repeat the law of conservation of matter. When you cook dinner, repeat the law of conservation of matter. There are examples all around us.

APPLY IT

Study Isaiah 40:12, Nehemiah 9:6, 2 Peter 3:7, and Hebrews 1:3.

How is the law of conservation of matter implied in these verses?

GO BEYOND

- Allow students to design an experiment to show the law of conservation of matter using a small kitchen scale, seltzer tablet, water, a balloon, and small mouth bottle.

- Watch a movie which defies the law of conservation of matter, such as *Honey I Shrunk the Kids* or *Despicable Me*. Discuss how although it is theoretically possible to condense matter, it cannot be destroyed. Therefore, although the object is smaller, it would have the same mass.

- Do a character study of "the father of modern chemistry," Antoine Lavoisier (1743-1794).

- Study "The Feeding of the 4,000" in Mark 8:1-9 and Matthew 15:32-39.

- Research how the abundance of elements in the human body are similar to the abundance of elements in the earth's crust and atmosphere. How does this prove Genesis 2:7 and Ecclesiastes 3:20?

CONSERVATION OF MATTER

INDICATIONS OF A CHEMICAL REACTION

Objectives: Learn the four indications that a chemical change has occurred. Explore examples of each indication. Identify chemical reactions beyond the classroom.

MATERIALS

1. Baking soda
2. Vinegar
3. Plaster of Paris
4. Candle
5. A match
6. A nail and a rusted nail
7. Some dirty pennies
8. Dark cola
9. Empty soda bottle (16 oz.)
10. A half cup hydrogen peroxide
11. Dish washing soap
12. 1 package baking yeast
13. Warm water
14. A cup
15. A blind fold

Romans 1:20 tells us that, "Since the creation of the world God's invisible qualities—his eternal power and divine nature—have been clearly seen, being understood from what has been made, so that people are without excuse."

BIG IDEA

What are some ways you know God exists? Beautiful planet, people's love for each other, the human imagination, God's love for us, miracles, amazing plants and animals, what Jesus did for us, the Holy Spirit's pursuit of our hearts, etc.

Some of these things we can see and some of these things we cannot see. What are some things you *can* see that show you that God exists? What are some things you *cannot* see that show you that God exists?

God created our world full of tiny little atoms. We cannot see them because they are so tiny, but they do exist. You are made of atoms, the table is made of atoms, even the air is made of atoms. They are like building blocks for everything in God's creation. These atoms move, change, and interact. When they do, it is called a CHEMICAL REACTION. There are 4 ways you know for sure that a chemical reaction has occurred:

1. Color change – like leaves in the fall, burning toast.
   Can you think of any other color changes?

CHEMICAL REACTION

2. Production of a gas or odor – like bread dough rising, stinky garbage rotting, the smell of smoke. Can you think of any other things that produce a gas or odor?

3. Production of heat or light – fire, glow stick. Can you think of any other things that produce heat or light?

CHEMICAL REACTION

4. Formation of a solid (precipitate) – this is more difficult to identify. Like concrete hardening.

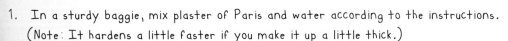

PLASTER OF PARIS:

ACTIVITY 1

1. In a sturdy baggie, mix plaster of Paris and water according to the instructions. (Note: It hardens a little faster if you make it up a little thick.)

2. Let the students feel the mixture. Set it aside. The student should touch the mixture every few minutes because it goes through a noticeable "heat" during the hardening process. Examine the baggie at the end of the other activities.

3. Did a chemical reaction occur? (Yes, formation of a solid and the production of heat)

ACTIVITY 2

CANDLE:

1. Strike the match. Ask, "Is a chemical reaction occurring?" (Yes: heat and light)

2. Light the candle. Ask, "Is a chemical reaction occurring?" (Yes: production of CO_2 gas, heat, and light)

3. Blow out the match. Let the students examine the smoldering match. Ask, "Has a chemical reaction occurred?" (Yes: color change, production of a gas, smoke)

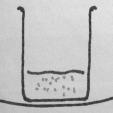

BAKING SODA AND VINEGAR:

ACTIVITY 3

1. In a clear container mix a little baking soda and vinegar. It is a good idea to do this on a plate because it may overflow the container.

2. Ask, "Is a chemical reaction occurring?" (Yes: production of a gas)

CLEAN A PENNY:

1. Pour a little dark soda in a cup. Allow the students to examine a dirty penny.

2. Place the penny in the soda. Slosh it around; rub it a little.

3. Remove the penny from the soda. Ask, "Did a chemical reaction occur?"
   (Yes: color change)

HYDROGEN PEROXIDE AND YEAST:

1. In the cup, mix the package of baking yeast and warm water. Mix it gently, and set it aside during steps 2 and 3.

2. Place the half cup of hydrogen peroxide in the plastic bottle.

3. Add about a tablespoon of dish soap to the hydrogen peroxide in the plastic bottle. Swirl the bottle to mix. Do not violently shake it.

4. Pour the yeast/water mixture into the bottle with the hydrogen peroxide/soap mixture. It is a good idea to do this on a plate because it will overflow the container.

5. When the reaction is complete, ask students to touch the plastic bottle.

6. Ask, "Did a chemical reaction occur?" (Yes: production of a gas, production of heat)

BLIND FAITH:

1. John 20:29 says, Then Jesus told him, "Because you have seen me, you have believed; blessed are those who have not seen and yet have believed." What do you think this means?

   a. We are to believe in Jesus and obey His commands, even though we cannot see him.

2. Blindfold one child. Instruct him/her that an obstacle will be placed in the room, but he/she will be safe as long as the instructions are followed.

3. Place a table or chair or table in the center of the room. Tell the child to listen carefully and walk across the room.

4. As the child walks, give him/her instructions like, "Crawl under the table." or, "Walk left around the chair."

5. When the child reaches the opposite side of the room and has removed the blindfold, ask, "How did you know how to get around the obstacle?" This is like faith, believing without seeing. Faith is a wonderful gift from God.

6. Say a prayer for God to give each child great faith.

- Although the atoms of the chemical reactions are too small to see, the chemical reaction is definitely visible. Remember Romans 1:20 tells us that, "since the creation of the world God's invisible qualities—his eternal power and divine nature—have been clearly seen, being understood from what has been made, so that people are without excuse." Although we cannot see Jesus, there is amazing evidence of His existence.

APPLY IT

- Chemical reactions occur all around us every day. Look for them as you go through life with your child:

  - o Almost all cooking is a chemical reaction – batters become solid, meat changes color, bread rises, eggs cook to a solid, cut fruit changes color over time, etc.
  - o Touch the hood of a car that has been running to feel the heat produced by the burning gasoline.
  - o Watch the leaves change color in the fall; see a colorful flower bloom from a green plant.
  - o Smell the production of gases from food cooking, car exhaust, and stinky garbage.

- John 20:29 says, Then Jesus told him, "Because you have seen me, you have believed; blessed are those who have not seen and yet have believed." Although we have not seen Jesus, we are called to believe. Look around for evidence of Jesus' existence and love.

- Drop a few regular Mentos into a 2 L bottle of Diet Coke; be prepared to run. Observe evidence of a chemical reaction. (Note: Perform this activity outside on an easy to clean surface.)

GO BEYOND

- Allow your student to design and execute an experiment to determine how to best clean dirty pennies (Mustard? Milk? Other soda? Etc.) Observe the evidence of a chemical reaction.

- Study the difference between a chemical reaction and a physical change.

CHEMICAL REACTION

HEAT CAPACITY AND SPECIFIC HEAT

Objectives: Understand the meaning of heat capacity. Apply the concept of heat capacity to various foods. Understand the meaning of specific heat. Apply the concept of specific heat to various foods.

Have you ever burned your mouth on hot food? (pizza, soup, noodles, etc.)

BIG IDEA

How can you get your food to cool so you can eat it? (blow on it, cut it into smaller pieces, wait etc.)

Hazards: Do not eat the foods until they cool completely. If your child is too young to discriminate between warm and hot foods, simply use warm food for this experiment. Make sure hands are washed before touching food.

MATERIALS

1. A cooked meal with hot food (this can be done at meal time)
2. One coffee cup for each child (of various styles, conditions, sizes, prettiness)
3. Hot chocolate
4. Cold milk

[Note: The beverage choices can be altered to account for food allergies or preference. It's the temperature that is important.]

HEAT CAPACITY:

ACTIVITY 1

1. At the dinner table, present your child with two hot pieces of the same food. One piece fairly small, the other piece rather large.

2. Form a hypothesis: Which piece will cool faster? Why?
3. Test the hypothesis by cautiously touching the two pieces of food periodically.
4. The smaller piece cools faster because it has a **lower heat capacity**. That means it stores less heat. The larger piece stays warm because it has a **higher heat capacity**. That means it stores more heat. Therefore, the smaller piece of food has less heat stored, so it becomes cool quicker.

SPECIFIC HEAT:

1. At the dinner table, present your child with two same-size hot pieces of different foods. (Perhaps a bite of potato and a bite of meat.)

2. Form a hypothesis: Which piece will cool faster?

3. Test the hypothesis by cautiously touching the two pieces of food periodically.

4. Various foods have different rates of cooling. Some foods cool off very fast, while some stay hot for a long time. If a food cools quickly (like meats and bread), it has a low specific heat. If a food stays hot (like cheese or soup) for an extended time, it has a high specific heat. God created different materials with different specific heats that are "specific" for those materials.

HOT CHOCOLATE:

1. Prepare coffee cups half full of hot chocolate. Place the wide variety of cups in the center of the table. Warn the children that the cups are HOT; they have a high specific heat. Tell the children not to touch the cups, but to look at the cups and quietly choose which cup they want.

2. Tell the children that the hot chocolate is it too hot to drink. How can it be cooled down? Wait for it to cool, add milk, add ice. Add milk to each cup of chocolate so they are safely cooled to drink.

3. Go around the table, one student at a time (perhaps youngest to oldest.) Allow each child to pick his/her favorite cup. There will inevitably be conflicts between children who both wanted the same cup. Allow these conflicts to play out and/or escalate for a few moments. Take care not to allow children to grab cups from each other's hands.

   - Notice that all of the pretty cups were taken first, leaving the ugly ones behind. Does the appearance of the cup add anything to the goodness of the hot chocolate?

4. Life is like the hot chocolate; while school, money, clothes, sports, and chores are like the cup. The cup does not change the quality of the hot chocolate. Just as the circumstances around you do not change the joy in your life. If we concentrate on the cup, we will forget all about enjoying the hot chocolate.

   - God is the creator of life (the hot chocolate); people choose what they put around their lives (the cup). The happiest people may not be on the best sports teams, may not have the best cars, may not go to the best schools, may not own the nicest houses, nor drive the most expensive cars. The happiest people make the best of what they have; they enjoy the life God gave them, regardless of the cup.

1 Thessalonians 5:16-18 tells us to, "Rejoice always, pray continually, give thanks in all circumstances; for this is God's will for you in Christ Jesus."

HEAT CAPACITY

5. Add milk to cool the hot chocolate and enjoy drinking it, no matter how pretty the cup is.

HEAT CAPACITY

- On a cold day, notice that a puddle freezes while a lake does not. They are both water (same specific heat), but the puddle has lower heat capacity because it has less mass. The lake has higher heat capacity because it has more mass.

- On a warm day, notice that a puddle becomes quite hot while a lake does not. They are both water (same specific heat), but the puddle has less mass, therefore it warms much more quickly.

- Read the story of Paul and Silas in prison in Acts 16:16-40, especially focusing on verse 25.

- Make two lists, one labeled "hot chocolate" and one labeled "cup". Have the children write or draw aspects of their lives that fall into these two categories. For instance, "Hot Chocolate" may include family, joy, friends, laughter, the Bible, prayer, etc. "Cup" may include clothes, school, toys, sports, etc. Encourage the children to focus on the wonderful life God gave them, not the extra things that surround that life.

HOT CHOCOLATE	CUP

GO BEYOND

How Much Heat Can it Hold?

Objective: Measure the temperature change of two volumes of hot water over time.

ACTIVITY

MATERIALS
1. Two thermometers, 2. Two identical cups 3. Hot water.

1. Fill one cup full of hot water. Fill the other cup half full of hot water.

2. Measure and record the two temperatures.

3. Form a hypothesis: Which cup of water will cool quicker?

4. Five minutes later, record the two temperatures again.

5. Repeat every five minutes until attention spans wane.

6. Which volume cooled faster? Answer in terms of heat capacity.

CONDENSATION

Understand the process of condensation. Experiment with the source of condensation. Explore how temperature effects condensation.

MATERIALS

1. A sheep's wool or wool fabric (optional)
2. Three ice cold bottles of water
3. A towel, a gallon-sized zip-closing bag
4. Two clear cups per student
5. Hot tap water
6. Tape
7. A magnifying glass (optional)
8. An ice cube

[Note: This experiment works best in a moderately to very humid environment. If you have an arid climate, turn on a humidifier in the room to see more dramatic results.]

Place an ice cold bottle of water on the table in front of the students. Wipe it dry. Let it sit while you explain condensation.

Did you know that our air is really a mixture of several different things? What do you think is in our air? Water molecules are one of the ingredients floating all around you right now. You cannot see them when

BIG IDEA

they are in the air, but we can coax them out of the air into liquid form. Examine the bottle of water. Notice how it is wet on the outside. This water did not leak out of the bottle through the plastic. The water came out of the air and stuck to the cold sides of the bottle.

The cold bottle decreases the temperature of the air around it. The water vapor molecules move slower and slower as they cool. When they are moving slowly enough, they cling together and change from a gas in the air to a liquid on the outside of the bottle.

- Ask the students to stand up and jump around. This is how water molecules behave when they are a gas (water vapor).
- Then ask the students to hold hands and jog in place. This is how water molecules behave when they are a liquid.

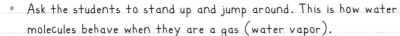

Condensation is when the water turns from water vapor (gas) into liquid water as it cools.

Pass the wool around for the students to feel while you read the following Bible story. Judges 6:36–38 tells a story about condensation.

CONDENSATION

CONDENSATION

Gideon said to God, "If you will save Israel by my hand as you have promised — look, I will place a wool fleece on the threshing floor. If there is dew only on the fleece and all the ground is dry, then I will know that you will save Israel by my hand, as you said." And that is what happened. Gideon rose early the next day; he squeezed the fleece and wrung out the dew — a bowlful of water.

Then Gideon said to God, "Do not be angry with me. Let me make just one more request. Allow me one more test with the fleece, but this time make the fleece dry and let the ground be covered with dew." That night God did so. Only the fleece was dry; all the ground was covered with dew.

Gideon was not born a warrior, but God had commanded him to fight for Israel. Do you think he was scared? Gideon wanted to make sure God really wanted him to save Israel from their enemies, the Midianites and Amalekites. So he asked God for affirmation using the fleece. We should always trust God when we are scared. God may ask us to do some difficult things, and we may not feel like we are good enough or strong enough to obey God.

Philippians 4:13 is a reminder that "I can do all things through [Christ] who gives me strength."

Has God ever asked you to do something difficult?

What is the condensation in this story? (The dew; the water vapor in the air formed condensation first on fleece and then on the ground.)

BOTTLE IN A BAG:

ACTIVITY 1

1. Place two identical, ice cold bottles of water in front of the students.

2. Dry them off thoroughly.

3. Immediately, place one bottle in the plastic baggie. Squeeze as much air out as possible and seal the baggie tightly.

4. Form a hypothesis: Which bottle will collect the most condensation?

5. Allow the bottles to sit for about 5 minutes. Examine the bottles.

6. The bottle inside the baggie has less moisture because not much air was able to contact it. Therefore, not much water vapor was able to condense. The bottle sitting out in the air had contact with plenty of water vapor, thus creating more condensation.

CUP TRAP:

1. Fill one of the clear plastic cups about half full of hot tap water.

2. Place the other plastic cup upside down on the rim of the cup containing hot water. Tape around the edge to stabilize.

3. Form a hypothesis: What will happen to the water in the bottom cup?

4. Observe the cups for about 2 minutes.

5. Use the magnifying glass to examine the sides of the top cup.

6. Remove the top cup and feel the inside surface.

7. What is on the inside of the top cup? (condensation). How did the condensation get there? (Some of the hot water evaporated into the air, then hit the cooler plastic of the top cup, and formed condensation)

8. Repeat this experiment using two cups of hot water covered by two cups to collect the condensation. But this time place an ice cube on the upturned bottom of one of the collection cups.

Did this change the amount of condensation? How does temperature affect the rate of condensation? (Cooler temperatures slow the motion of the water vapor molecules, causing them to turn into liquid, creating more condensation faster).

- Collect several pieces of wool and wool fabrics. Allow students to experiment with making them wet and dry as in the story of Gideon.

- Point out that clouds are big examples of condensation.

- Write Philippians 4:13 in the condensation of a bathroom mirror after a steamy shower.

- Fog up a cool window or mirror with your breath.

- Observe how warm breath condenses in the air in cold weather.

- Study the opposite of condensation, evaporation: the phase change from liquid to gas. Study condensation and evaporation in relation to the water cycle.

PURE DRINKING WATER USING CONDENSATION:

MATERIALS
1. Two plastic cups
2. Hot tap water
3. Food coloring
4. Ice cube
5. White paper towel

1. Fill a clear plastic cup half full of hot tap water. Add one or two drops of food coloring to the hot water and stir.

2. Turn the other clear plastic cup upside down on top of the cup containing the hot water. Place the ice cube on the upturned bottom to speed condensation.

3. Wait about 2 minutes. Use the white paper towel to wipe the inside surface of the top cup. Is there any color in it? (The processes of evaporation and condensation have deposited only pure water in the upper cup, not the dye.)

When I look at your heavens,
the work of your fingers,

the moon and the stars,
which you have set in place,

what is man that you are
mindful of him,

and the son of man
that you care for him?

Psalm 8:3-4

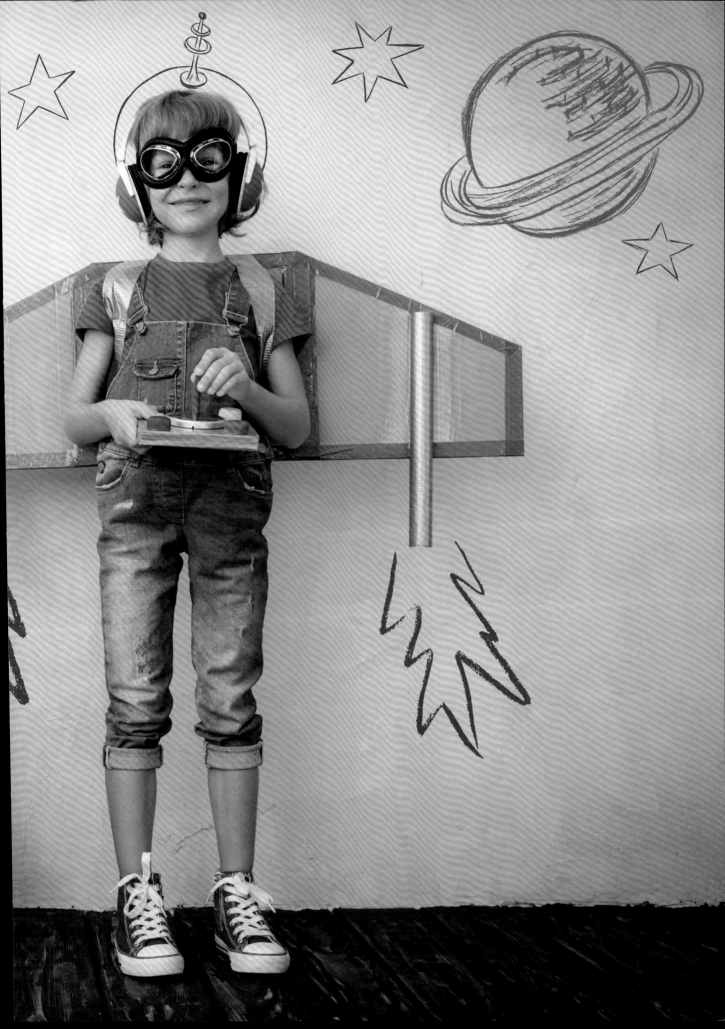

COLLIGATIVE PROPERTIES

Objectives: Observe the approximate rate of freezing of salt water and fresh water. Understand the colligative property responsible for this difference.

MATERIALS

1. A globe or map
2. 2 identical plastic cups
3. A measuring cup
4. Water
5. Salt
6. A pot to boil water
7. A time keeping device
8. Freezer
9. Stove top

In Genesis 1:9-10 (CEV), God said, "I command the water under the sky to come together in one place, so there will be dry ground." And that's what happened. God named the dry ground "Land," and he named the water "Ocean." God looked at what he had done and saw that it was good.

BIG IDEA

God created some of the water on earth to be salt water, and some to be fresh water. Where can salt water be found? (Oceans and seas) Where can fresh water be found? (lakes, rivers, ground water). Examine the globe. Notice how much of the globe is water and how much is land. Find fresh water lakes and rivers. Find salt water oceans and seas. Ask the children to point out bodies of fresh water and salt water on the globe. Ask them to close their eyes while you spin the globe. Then ask them to blindly touch the globe. Then they can open their eyes to see if they touched land, salt water, or fresh water. Older children can keep a chart to record how many times each location was touched.

God was very intentional as he placed the salt water in oceans and the fresh water in lakes and streams. God created salt water and fresh water to act differently. The word for this in chemistry is **colligative properties**. This refers to how water boils, freezes, or evaporates. All of these things depend on how much salt (or any other solute) is in the water (solvent).

> Today we are going to explore a few differences in salt water and fresh water.

COLLIGATIVE PROPERTIES

FREEZING POINT DEPRESSION:

1. Label the plastic cups "fresh water" and "salt water".

2. Measure 1/4 cup of water into each of the two plastic cups.

3. Slowly add salt to the "salt water" cup while stirring. When the salt stops dissolving, stop adding; the solution is saturated.

   a. A saturated solution has visible salt crystals that are not dissolving. If any more salt is added, it settles to the bottom or swirls around as the solution is stirred.

   b. Allow children to dip their finger into the salt water and fresh water to taste.

4. Form a hypothesis: Which one will freeze first?

5. Place both cups in a similar position in the freezer.

6. Continue on to Activity 2. Check to see if the water in either cup is beginning to freeze in about 30 minutes. If not, check again after an hour has passed.

7. The fresh water freezes first because the salt dissolved in the salt water gets in the way of the ice crystals trying to form. Therefore, it requires a lower temperature to freeze salty water; this is called freezing point depression.

   a. Here is an analogy to share: The fresh water in the cup is like a room full of children (representing the liquid water molecules). When the teacher says, "Line up as fast as you can!" the children can line up very fast (representing freezing). The salt water in the cup is like a room full of children *and* big bouncy balls (representing the salt). When the teacher says, "Line up as fast as you can!" the children have to make their way around all of the bouncy balls to form a line. It is much more difficult; the balls keep getting in the way and bumping kids out of line.

FREEZING POINT ELEVATION:

[WARNING - BOILING WATER AND HOT STOVE ARE NEEDED FOR THIS ACTIVITY. USE CARE WITH YOUNG CHILDREN.]

1. Pre-heat a burner on the stove to the highest temperature setting.

2. Measure one cup of water into the cool pot.

3. After the burner has reached its maximum temperature, place the pot of water on the hot stove and start timing.

4. When the water reaches a rolling boil, stop time. Record how many minutes it took for the one cup of fresh water to boil.

5. Empty pot and let it cool while you prepare the salt water.

ACTIVITY
2
CONTINUED...

6. Measure one cup of water in the measuring cup.

7. Slowly add salt while stirring. When the salt stops dissolving, stop adding; the solution is saturated.

8. Form a hypothesis: Will the salt water take more or less time to reach boiling?

9. Pour the salt water solution into the cool pot, and place it on the pre-heated stove and start timing.

10. When the water reaches a rolling boil, stop time. Record how many minutes it took for the one cup of salt water to boil.

11. The fresh water boils first. It also boils at a lower temperature. This is because the salt dissolved in the salt water gets in the way of the water molecules as they go from liquid to gas.

   a. Here is an analogy to share: The fresh water is like a room full of children (representing the liquid water molecules). When the teacher says, "Get out of the room as fast as you can!" the children can get out very fast (representing boiling). The salt water is like a room full of children and big bouncy balls (representing the salt). When the teacher says, "Get out of the room as fast as you can!" the children have to make their way around all of the bouncy balls to get out the door. It is much more difficult; the balls keep getting in the way and slowing kids down.

- **Vapor Pressure Lowering** is the third colligative property. Design and perform an experiment to test the rate of evaporation of salt versus fresh water.

- Question: Why do you think God made the oceans salty? They do not easily boil, they do not easily freeze, and they do not easily evaporate.

- Question: The polar ice caps are mostly frozen fresh water, in a salty sea. Why?

APPLY IT

Answers:

   o Salt water has a lower freezing point than fresh water. Therefore, it has to be colder to freeze the salt water.

   o Snow pack makes up much of the ice caps. Snow falls as frozen fresh water, then is compacted into ice.

   o If the temperature drops low enough to freeze salt water from the sea, the salt leaches out over time leaving behind very firm fresh water ice.

- Question: If you add salt to water before eggs are boiled, the eggs cook faster. Why?

   Answer: It is a common misconception that adding salt to water makes it boil faster. Actually, the salt water boils more slowly, but at a higher temperature. Thus, cooking the food faster.

COLLIGATIVE PROPERTIES

GO BEYOND

- There are many interesting facts about earth's water at http://water.usgs.gov/edu/earthhowmuch.html

- The colligative properties of solutions depend on how much solute is in the solvent, but the *type* of solute is not important. Perform the above experiments again with sugar instead of salt. Are the results the same?

MORE SCIENCE: OSMOSIS

COLLIGATIVE
PROPERTIES

OSMOTIC PRESSURE

Osmotic Pressure is the fourth colligative property. It is more difficult to explain, but simple to observe. Osmosis is the process of water molecules passing through a semipermeable membrane. The water molecules move from the less concentrated solution to the more concentrated solution, therefore balancing the concentrations on either side of the membrane. Osmosis in plants is caused when water passes through the cell wall. It is called turgor pressure or hydrostatic pressure.

CHERRY OSMOSIS

Place a cherry in a bowl of water over night. What happens?

ACTIVITY 1

   The cherry soaks water in through the skin (semipermeable membrane) by osmosis. Water always moves in a direction to dilute the solute (in this case fructose). The water builds up osmotic pressure inside the cherry until sometimes the cherry bursts. This is a problem for cherry farmers on rainy days.

ACTIVITY 2

POTATO OSMOSIS

- Place the plates on a flat, stable surface. Fill both plates with water. Add a couple of tablespoons of salt to one plate. Label that plate "salt water"; label the other plate "water".

MATERIALS

- Observe the halved potato. Notice the color, texture, and firmness. Place the two halves, face down, on the two plates. Let them soak for two to three hours.

1. A potato cut in half,
2. Two plates,
3. Salt,
4. Water

- Flip the potatoes face up and observe.

  o The potato half that soaked in fresh water will appear about the same. Upon close observation, you will notice it is more rigid. This is because there are more salts and minerals in the potato than there are in the fresh water. Therefore, water will move into the potato cells (from the less concentrated solution in the plate, to the more concentrated solution in the potato cells). The potato cell walls serve as the semipermeable membrane.

  o The potato half that soaked in salt water appears very different. How would you describe it? Wilted, soft, flexible. This is because there is more salt in the plate than there is in the potato. Therefore, water will move out of the potato cells (from the less concentrated solution inside the potato cells, to the more concentrated solution in the plate). The cells lose their turgor pressure, like balloons losing their air.

Salt Water

water

SYMMETRY IN NATURE

Objective: Identify and understand linear and radial symmetry. Observe examples of symmetry in nature. Draw images that are radially and linearly symmetrical.

MATERIALS

1. Several pictures of butterflies with their wings spread
2. Several daisy type flowers or pictures of flowers
3. White cardstock
4. Scissors
5. Paint
6. Paintbrushes
7. At least one empty toilet paper roll per child
8. White note cards
9. Scissors
10. Glue

Colossians 1:16 - 17 reminds us that "In [the Son] all things were created: things in heaven and on earth, visible and invisible ... all things have been created through Him and for Him. He is before all things, and in Him all things hold together."

BIG IDEA

God made so many beautiful things. What are some things you find beautiful in nature?

We are going to take a look at a few particularly beautiful things today. Place a picture of a butterfly before the children. Ask, "What do you observe about this butterfly?" (pretty, colorful, insect, wings, etc.) Do you notice that both wings are the same? Every single detail of one wing is replicated on the other wing. This is called **symmetry**. God made symmetry everywhere in nature. If you divide something in half, you will often find that the two halves are the same. This is called **linear symmetry** (also known as bilateral symmetry). Think of your own body; is it symmetrical? Draw an imaginary line from your forehead, straight through your nose, down to your belly button. Each side has one eye, one ear, one arm, one leg, 5 fingers, 5 toes, etc.

Place a flower in front of the children. Is this symmetrical? A flower is an example of **radial symmetry**. If you turn the flower around on the axis created by its stem, does it look the same? What are some other examples of radial symmetry? (bike wheel, starfish, jelly fish)

SYMMETRY IN NATURE

LINEAR SYMMETRY BUTTERFLY:

SYMMETRY IN NATURE

ACTIVITY 1

1. Fold a piece of paper in half crossways.

2. Cut out half of a butterfly shape, with the body toward the fold. Cut through both layers of paper.

3. Unfold the paper and lay the butterfly shape flat. Ask the students, what kind of symmetry does this butterfly have? (linear)

4. Using plenty of paint, smear colors all over the butterfly. Explain to the children to not put too much time into the details. It is fine to leave some white spots.

5. Before the paint has time to begin to dry, fold the butterfly back in half with the paint on the inside. Press the wings together completely.

6. Unfold the butterfly and allow it to dry. It will have great linear symmetry.

RADIAL SYMMETRY FLOWERS:

ACTIVITY 2

1. Cut each toilet paper roll into three round sections. Younger children may need help with this step.

2. Cut slits into the edge of each piece, but do not cut all the way through.

3. Fan out the cardboard to make petals.

4. Paint the petals in any pattern. Allow children to make as many flowers as they wish. Encourage variation on number of petals and pattern of paint.

5. Outline the bottom edges of the toilet paper flowers with glue and place them near the tops of the note cards. Allow glue to dry completely, perhaps overnight.

6. Draw in stems, leaves, and centers to complete the flowers. These beauties have radial symmetry!

NATURE WALK:

ACTIVITY 3

1. Go outside and search for examples of linear and radial symmetry.

a. Examples of linear symmetry may include leaves, insects, lizards, squirrels, fish, ducks, etc.

b. Examples of radial symmetry may include flowers, fruits cut in cross section, seeds, spider webs, etc.

- Create an art garden by fastening the flowers and butterflies from activities 1 and 2 to a bulletin board or wall. Ask the children to draw or paint some of the symmetrical objects they observed on their nature walk. Add them to the garden.

- Look for examples of symmetry as you go through the week: cars, chairs, foods, etc.

SYMMETRICAL SNACKS:

- Use snack time to review Colossians 1:17 "He is before all things, and in Him all things hold together."

  o Cut two apples in half, one vertically (from the stem down) and one horizontally (across the middle). Which apple shows linear symmetry? Which apple shows radial symmetry?

  o Many round crackers and cookies have radial symmetry.

  o What kind of symmetry does a carrot have?

  o How about a cucumber cut into round slices?

  o Do Goldfish crackers have symmetry?

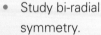

- Why do humans like symmetry so much?
- Study the images created by a kaleidoscope. What type of symmetry does a kaleidoscope demonstrate?
- Study bi-radial symmetry.

SYMMETRY IN NATURE

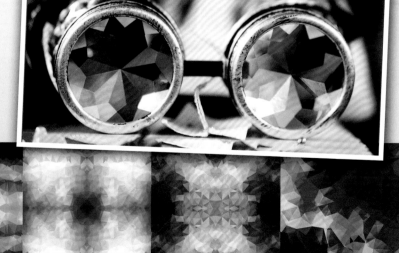

Deciduous and Evergreen Trees

Objective: Learn the differences between basic deciduous and evergreen trees. Identify local deciduous, conifer, and palm trees.

Isaiah 41:17-20

"The poor and needy search for water, but there is none; their tongues are parched with thirst. But I the Lord will answer them; I, the God of Israel, will not forsake them. I will make rivers flow on barren heights, and springs within the valleys. I will turn the desert into pools of water, and the parched ground into springs. I will put in the desert the cedar and the acacia, the myrtle and the olive. I will set junipers in the wasteland, the fir and the cypress together, so that people may see and know, may consider and understand, that the hand of the Lord has done this, that the Holy One of Israel has created it."

God's people were in the hot, dry Arabia Desert. This place is a vast, parched plain. It is filled with burning sand and barren rocks.

- How do you think the people felt? Thirsty, hot, maybe lost or forgotten.

- With what did God supply them? Water and trees. The water was to quench their thirst, but what were the trees for? God provided the tallest and most beautiful trees to furnish shade and protection. God's grace provided for their human needs.

- Can you imagine being in the middle of a huge desert, thirsty and hot? Now, can you imagine seeing water spring up out of the dry sand and groves of trees grow tall before your eyes?

- All of the trees mentioned are shade trees, but they do not usually grow together. This is a picture of God's miraculous power to provide for His people.

- What are some ways we use trees? Wood for houses and furniture, fruit for food, shade and beauty for yards, etc.

- God wants to meet the needs of all of His people. When our need is greatest, His grace is abundant.

Today, we are going to learn about the different types of trees.

MATERIALS

1. A forest consisting of a mixture of tree species in fall or winter

2. One piece of white poster board

3. Green construction paper cut into the shape of leaves about 6 inches long

DECIDUOUS AND EVERGREEN TREES

TREES

RIGHTEOUS TREE:

ACTIVITY
1

1. Examine a large, healthy tree. A photograph will suffice. How did this tree grow so large? (time, water, sun, carbon dioxide, soil, etc.) Just as the tree needs these elements to thrive, we need certain things to grow to be more like Jesus.

2. Draw a large, leafless tree trunk and branches on the poster board. This tree is like a person who has put their faith in Jesus. We are going to search Psalm 1 for characteristics of a righteous person.

3. Instruct the children to listen quietly while you read Psalm 1 the first time. Then ask them to point out **the traits of a righteous person** as you read it a second time.

Psalm 1

Blessed is the one who *does not walk in step with the wicked or stand in the way that sinners take or sit in the company of mockers,* but whose delight is in the law of the Lord, and who meditates on his law day and night. That person is like a tree planted by streams of water, *which yields its fruit in season* and whose *leaf does not wither –* whatever they do *prospers.*
Not so the wicked! They are like chaff that the wind blows away. Therefore the wicked will not stand in the judgment, nor sinners in the assembly of the righteous. *For the Lord watches over the way of the righteous,* but the way of the wicked leads to destruction.

4. When a child gives an answer, write it on one of the pre-cut leaves. Glue or tape it to the tree branches.

5. As a leaf is added, discuss its meaning. Also, consider examples of how these traits can be applied to the lives of the children. Make leaves for these applications as well.

6. Write Psalm 1:3 on the trunk of the tree.

Psalm 1:3 [The righteous] person is like a tree planted by streams of water, which yields its fruit in season and whose leaf does not wither—whatever they do prospers.

TREE IDENTIFICATION:

ACTIVITY
2

1. There are so many different kinds of trees on our earth, but all of them can fit into three categories.

2. Look around, can you see trees that are green?

3. Can you see trees without leaves (or with brown, yellow, orange, or red leaves)?
You have just spotted two of the basic kinds of trees.

   a. The trees that stay green through the winter are called **evergreen**. They are "forever green." Evergreen trees actually do lose leaves, but not all at the same time the way that deciduous trees do. Evergreen trees use their leaves through the winter to do photosynthesis.

   b. The trees that lose their leaves in the winter are called **deciduous**. The word deciduous means "falling down." In the winter, deciduous trees shed their leaves because there is not enough light or water to make photosynthesis worthwhile. Therefore, the leaves change from green to red, yellow, orange or brown. Then the leaves fall to the ground, and the tree goes dormant, like a deep sleep.

c. The third category is **palm** trees. These usually only grow in tropical areas (USDA zones 8-10).

   i. They may have fan shaped leaves (palmate) or feather shaped leaves (pinnate).

   ii. Some types of palm trees grow coconuts. Others grow dates or other various palm fruits.

   iii. The trunk of the palm tree does not have annual rings, but rather tough vertical fibers.

NOTE: Trees often grow very differently in the tropics. Because there is no winter season, even deciduous trees may stay green year around. However, the trees can easily be identified as needleleaf (evergreen), broadleaf (deciduous), or palm (see table below).

4. Continue to explore with the students, pointing out evergreen and deciduous trees and shrubs.

The following table is a list of terms commonly used to refer to deciduous and evergreen trees. There are some exceptions; see "Go Beyond" section.

Deciduous	Evergreen
Deciduous = drop their leaves in winter. The word deciduous means "to fall down" in Latin.  Examples: Maple, oak, hickory, cherry tree, elm, beach, chestnut, birch, dogwood	Evergreen = keep their leaves year around. Coniferous = bear seeds in cones, most conifers are evergreen. Examples: Pine, cedar, hemlock, spruce, fir, yew, juniper
Broadleaf = a leaf with a lot of surface area. 	Needleleaf = long thin leaf, typical of conifers.
Hardwood = a word commonly used for deciduous trees, although some many have softer wood.	Softwood = a word commonly used for conifers, although many have harder wood.
Angiosperm = any plant that produces flowers to make seeds; the seed is subsequently enclosed in a fruit. This includes flowering trees like crabapple, pear, and oak, as well as other plants like roses, clover, azaleas, and tomatoes. Palm trees are also angiosperm. Note: Many ornamental trees have been hybridized to bloom, but do not produce fruit.	Gymnosperm = any plant that produces "naked seeds", not enclosed in a fruit; many produce seeds in a cone. This includes cycads and ginkgoes as well as the typical needle leaf pine, spruce, and fir.

TREES

- Continue to identify evergreen and deciduous trees through the season. Use this as an opportunity to review Psalm 1:3.

> **Psalm 1:3** [The righteous] person is like a tree planted by streams of water, which yields its fruit in season and whose leaf does not wither—whatever they do prospers.

- Study the following verses to find references specifically to evergreen or deciduous trees:

Psalm 37:35

I have seen a wicked and ruthless man flourishing like a luxuriant native tree,

Jeremiah 17:2

Even their children remember their altars and Asherah poles

beside the spreading trees and on the high hills.

Isaiah 6:13

And though a tenth remains in the land,
it will again be laid waste.

But as the terebinth and oak leave stumps when they are cut down,

so the holy seed will be the stump in the land."

GO BEYOND

- Study the pagan history and symbolism of the evergreen as a Christmas tree.

- Read Isaiah 41:17-20 again. How many kinds of trees are listed? Seven. This is the number of perfection in the Bible. Find other examples of the number seven.

- Explore the advantages and disadvantages of a tree being evergreen or deciduous. More advanced students should examine the species found in various USDA zones, and explore why God placed those species in those locations.

- Find and/or study exceptions to normal tree classification. Here are a few examples:

DECIDUOUS AND EVERGREEN TREES

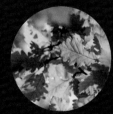

Live oak is a broadleaf evergreen.

The larch, bald cypress, and dawn redwood are deciduous conifers.

Many magnolia and holly trees are broadleaf evergreen.

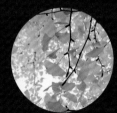

Ginkgo trees are broadleaf and deciduous, but they are gymnosperms.

MORE SCIENCE:

Why Leaves Change Color in the Fall:

All spring and summer, green chlorophyll in leaves is busy capturing sunlight to do photosynthesis. Photosynthesis, is the process by which plants make carbohydrates. These carbohydrates are nutrition for the plant, used to build stems, roots, bark, buds, and leaves.

As autumn comes, the days get shorter. Therefore, there is less light for photosynthesis. The trees begin to shut down their food making factories. The green chlorophyll disappears from the leaves. As the green fades, we can see yellow and orange. These colors have been in the leaves all spring and summer. We just couldn't see them because the green chlorophyll concealed them.

Another change occurs in the fall. At the point where the stem of the leaf is attached to the tree, a barrier (called the abscission layer) develops. The abscission layer gradually severs the tissue that supports the leaves. Thus, the nutrition flow is blocked from the twig to the leaf. When the leaf is blown by the wind it falls, leaving a sealed scar on the tree's twig. Some species of oaks do not create this barrier until spring begins again. They are easy to recognize because they are covered with brown leaves throughout the winter.

Chemical	Color	Trees
Xanthophylls	Yellow pigments	Aspen, honey locust, ash, beech
Carotenoids	Orange pigments	Sassafras, silver maple
Anthocyanins	Reds and purples (occurs when glucose is trapped in the leaves. The cool nights cause the glucose to turn red. The red and purple pigments are not usually in the leaf all season.)	Sugar maple, bald cypress, and many gum and oak trees
Tannins	Brown (the orange, yellow, and red pigments break down as temperatures drop below freezing, leaving behind the brown structure of the leaves).	Sugar maple, bald cypress, and many gum and oak trees

PLANT A BEAN

Objectives: Observe the sprouting and growth of a bean. Identify the parts of a plant. Understand the function of the parts of a plant.

MATERIALS

1. Bean seeds (dried grocery store beans work well: great northern, lima, or pinto)
2. Paper towels
3. Water
4. A clear glass jar with lid
5. Brown water-based paint
6. Green water-based paint
7. Paint brushes
8. Markers
9. Card stock
10. Plastic hollow coffee stirs or drinking straws

Genesis 1:11–13 Then God said, "Let the land produce vegetation: seed-bearing plants and trees on the land that bear fruit with seed in it, according to their various kinds." And it was so. The land produced vegetation: plants bearing seed according to their kinds and trees bearing fruit with seed in it according to their kinds. And God saw that it was good. And there was evening, and there was morning – the third day.

BIG IDEA

   Think of a world without plants. What would there be? Rocks, dirt, water? Think of all of the beautiful green leaves and colorful, fragrant flowers that existed by the end of the third day. The world went from a barren place, to a place filled with grass, leaves, stems, trunks, fruits, flowers, oxygen, shade, vines, etc. Furthermore, God created each plant to reproduce through its own seeds.

Give each child a bean. **Look** at these simple beans. Do you notice anything about the bean? (color, texture, size, etc.)

PLANT A BEAN

They look pretty simple. But God placed a great big secret inside every single bean. Today, we are going to begin to discover that secret. God is not in a hurry, so it will take several days to learn the secret. Can you be a patient learner?

BEAN SPROUTING:

Stem (epicotyl)
Leaf
Stem (hypocotyl)
Seed (cotyledon)
Root (radical)

ACTIVITY 1

1. Dampen several paper towels.

2. Place them loosely in the jar so that they press gently against the glass.

3. Place 2-4 beans around the outside of the paper towels; between the paper towels and the glass. Make sure the beans are not all the way to the bottom of the jar.

4. The seeds are **dormant**, which means they are alive, but not growing. Form a hypothesis: What will happen when the seeds have water, warmth, and air?

5. Loosely cap the lid to the jar and place in a warm location.

6. After 2 or 3 days, observe the beans. As the days pass, more and more parts of the plant will appear. The seeds **germinate**, which simply means they sprout. Check the paper towel periodically to make sure it remains moist.

   a. Notice which part of the plant emerges from the seed first? Why? The root emerges first to stabilize the seed and begin absorbing water and nutrients.

   b. Notice that the seed coat is no longer needed. It protected the seed when it was dormant, but as the seed absorbs water (imbition), the seed coat is cast off.

7. Identify the **seed** (cotyledon), **root** (radical), **stem** (epicotyl above the seed, hypocotyl below the seed), and **leaves**. Older children can use a sharpie to write the parts of the plant on the outside of the glass jar.

See God's secret? There was all of the information for a whole plant right inside that tiny bean!

SENSING GRAVITY:

ACTIVITY 2

1. After the beans have a nice sprout and root, turn the jar upside down.

2. Form a hypothesis: What will happen to the plant since it is turned upside down?

3. Observe the root and stem after 24 hours. Then again after 48 hours.

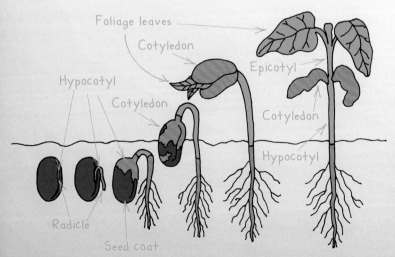

Foliage leaves
Cotyledon
Epicotyl
Hypocotyl
Cotyledon
Cotyledon
Hypocotyl
Radicle
Seed coat

4. How can this little plant "know" which way up is? It can sense gravity. The roots grow down and the stem grows up. Scientists do not yet fully understand how plants sense gravity. It is one of God's mysteries.

Note: Without soil and fresh air, the seedlings will eventually die. If you would like to continue to watch them grow, carefully transplant them to soil. Provide appropriate amounts of sunlight and water.

ROOTED IN HIS LOVE:

Ephesians 3:16-19 says, "I pray that out of his glorious riches he may strengthen you with power through his Spirit in your inner being, so that Christ may dwell in your hearts through faith. And I pray that you, *being rooted and established in love*, may have power, together with all the Lord's holy people, to grasp how wide and long and high and deep is the love of Christ, and to know this love that surpasses knowledge – that you may be filled to the measure of all the fullness of God.

1. Ask the children to paint a straight broad, brown line down the middle of their card stock. Then drip a half a tablespoon of watered down brown paint at one end of the line.

2. Have the students blow through the coffee stirrer on the watered down brown paint so the airflow pushes the paint down the paper, away from the broad line. Repeat this technique to have the children create several roots going down the page.

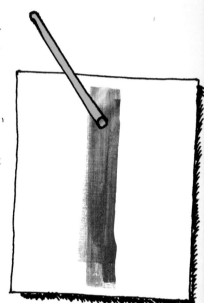

3. Let the paint dry for a few minutes. Now the plant is ready to decorate: leaves, flowers, insects, etc. Older children may wish to paint and label the leaf, stem, cotyledon, and root.

4. While the children decorate their plants, discuss how Christians are like a healthy plant:

   a. *Rooted* in the love of Christ. Colossians 2:7, Ephesians 3:17

   b. Produce *good fruit* and help others to grow in their faith. Psalm 1:3, Matthew 7:17

   c. *Do not worry* about the future. Jeremiah 17:8

   d. *Bring glory* to God. 1 Chronicles 16:33

   e. *Be strong* so we can help others. Romans 15:2, Joshua 1:9

APPLY IT

- Look for parts of plants in your world. When your child points out the roots of a plant, use this as an opportunity to summarize Ephesians 3:17 as "rooted in His love."

- Collect seeds and nuts from outside. Plant them to discover what plant they grow.

- What do you want to be when you grow up? You are like a seed, full of potential to become a big beautiful plant. To fulfill your purpose, nourish and unfold what God has already packed in.

  o *"Be a butcher if you want to, a sales rep if you like. Be an ambassador if you really care. You can be anything you want to be. If you work hard enough. But can you? If God didn't pack within you the meat sense of a butcher, the people skills of a salesperson, or the world vision of an ambassador, can you be one? An unhappy, dissatisfied one perhaps. But a fulfilled one? No. Can an acorn become a rose, a whale fly like a bird, or lead become gold? Absolutely not. You cannot be anything you want to be. But you can be everything God wants you to be?"* [1]

[1] Lucado, Max. *Cure for the Common Life*. Nashville, Tennessee: Thomas Nelson, 2005. p. 18.

PLANT A BEAN

- Study the plant experiment Thomas Andrew Knight did about 200 years ago. Can you replicate this experiment?
- Your child can keep a record of a bean's growth, either in the form of observations recorded in sentences or in the form of numerical data with which to create a line graph.
- Introduce the concept of DNA. God uses DNA to write the information to create every living thing, even a plant. A bean seed will never grow into an oak tree, as Genesis tells us "plants bearing seed according to their kinds."

GO BEYOND

MORE SCIENCE - PHOTOSYNTHESIS:

- In Latin, the word photosynthesis means "putting together with light."
- The balanced chemical equation is as follows:

$$6\,CO_2 + 6\,H_2O \xrightarrow{\text{sunlight}} C_6H_{12}O_6 + 6\,O_2$$

Carbon dioxide   Water   Glucose   Oxygen

- Carbon dioxide gas is taken in through **stomata**, tiny holes on the underside of the leaves.
- Water is absorbed by the roots and carried up to the leaves by **xylem vessels**, tiny tubes that transport water and minerals up the stem of a plant.
- The water and carbon dioxide make their way to individual, tiny plant cells. In all plant cells, there is an organelle called a **chloroplast**. Each plant cell contains between ten to one hundred chloroplasts. The chloroplasts contain the pigment **chlorophyll**. This amazing molecule absorbs energy from the sun.
- This energy is used by chlorophyll to split water molecules in to hydrogen and oxygen. The oxygen is released back out through the stomata as waste.
- The hydrogen is combined with the carbon dioxide from the atmosphere to make glucose, a simple sugar that serves as food for the plant.

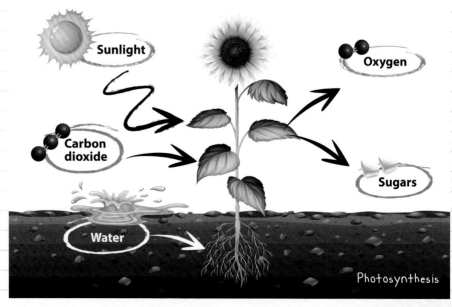

Sunlight

Oxygen

Carbon dioxide

Sugars

Water

Photosynthesis

Parts of a Plant
At the Dinner Table

Objectives: Identify edible leaves, roots, stems, seeds, and flowers.
Exposure to various foods. Review parts of a plant.

MATERIALS

Raw vegetables for a meal or salad which includes:

1. Leaves (lettuce, kale, or spinach)
2. Roots (carrots, radishes, or potatoes)
3. Stem (celery, asparagus, or rhubarb)
4. Seeds (peas, beans, corn, or nuts)
5. Flowers (broccoli, cauliflower, or artichoke)
6. Fruit (pear, apples, or strawberries)
7. Two similar pieces of fruit (one delicious and ripe; the other rotten)

Genesis 1:29-30

Then God said, "I give you every seed-bearing plant on the face of the whole earth and every tree that has fruit with seed in it. They will be yours for food. And to all the beasts of the earth and all the birds in the sky and all the creatures that move along the ground – everything that has the breath of life in it – I give every green plant for food." And it was so.

What are some of your favorite plants to eat? Isn't God a wonderful provider? He created all of the wonderful food for us to eat. God also gave plants for the animals to eat. What are some plants animals like to eat? Horses eat grass, rabbits eat carrots, giraffes eat leaves from trees, etc. Today, we are going to realize God's provision of plants for food.

BIG IDEA

ACTIVITY 1

Study the Food:

[Hazards: Take care with food preparation. Make sure hands are washed and sharp knives kept out of reach of young children.]

1. Place the uncut food before the children.
   For younger children, it may be best to show them the foods one at a time.
2. Examine the foods one by one, asking the children to identify which part of a plant they are.
3. As they identify the parts, discuss the function of each part:
   a. Roots – absorb minerals and water
   b. Stems – support the plant; carry water and nutrients up to the leaves
   c. Leaves – make food for the plant by photosynthesis
   d. Flowers – reproductive parts of the plant; contain ovule to make the seed
   e. Fruits – provide covering for the seed; can be hard or soft
   f. Seeds – contain the information and potential for a new plant; form in fruit

PARTS OF A PLANT

ACTIVITY 2 — PREPARE AND EAT THE FOOD

Discuss the meaning and purpose of plants in relation to Genesis 1:29-30 during your delicious meal.

FRUIT OF THE SPIRIT:

ACTIVITY 3

1. In Galatians 5:22-23, Paul tells us that "the fruit of the Spirit is love, joy, peace, forbearance, kindness, goodness, faithfulness, gentleness and self-control."

2. Pass the two similar pieces of fruit around the class, one delicious and the other rotten. Which piece of fruit would you eat? Why? How do they look? How do they smell? How do they feel?

3. The Holy Spirit makes his home in the hearts of believers. Do we grow fruit? We do not have apples and strawberries hanging off our arms. What do you think this verse means?

   a. Our spirits should grow a different kind of fruit: love, joy, peace, forbearance (patience), kindness, goodness, faithfulness, gentleness, and self-control.

   b. These are the good fruits that our lives should produce.

4. We are not perfect. If we are not following the Holy Spirit, our lives can produce bad fruit.

   a. What are some bad fruits in peoples' lives? Anger, selfishness, jealousy, being dishonest, hate, not putting God first (idolatry), fighting, etc.

5. Read the following scenarios out loud. Ask the children if they are an example of "good fruit" or "bad fruit."

a. Learning about God's Word.	Good fruit
b. Complaining about having to go to Church.	Bad fruit
c. Trusting God.	Good fruit
d. Not being angry at little sibling when he/she is destructive.	Good fruit
e. Fighting with your brother or sister.	Bad fruit
f. Helping Mom or Dad with yard work.	Good fruit
g. Playing video games all day.	Bad fruit
h. Singing to praise God.	Good fruit
i. Being friends with a new kid at school.	Good fruit
j. Teasing a kid at school.	Bad fruit
k. Being grouchy.	Bad fruit
l. Wanting what someone else has.	Bad fruit
m. Loving Jesus.	Good fruit

6. What makes the bad fruit bad? People's sinful nature and Satan's temptation. Bad trees make bad fruit.

7. What makes a good fruit good? God's grace, Jesus' sacrifice, forgiveness, and love. Good trees make good fruit.

8. What kind of fruit do you produce? Have you accepted Jesus and asked for forgiveness of your sin? Love Jesus; seek His kingdom, and grow in knowledge of Him. The Holy Spirit will help you produce good fruit.

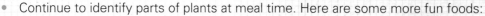

- Continue to identify parts of plants at meal time. Here are some more fun foods:

  o Bean sprouts (seed/stem)

  o Brussels sprouts (leaves)

  o Beets (root)

  o Eggplant (fruit)

  o Sunflower seeds (seed)

  o Bread (ground wheat seed)

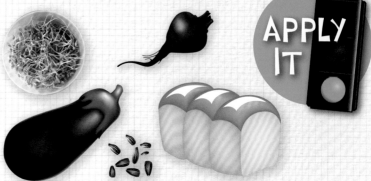

- In Matthew 12:33, Jesus says, "Make a tree good and its fruit will be good, or make a tree bad and its fruit will be bad, for a tree is recognized by its fruit." Let's think of how you are a good tree that makes good fruit.

  o Draw an outline of a tree on a blank sheet of paper.

  o As your children go through the week, notice good fruit like helping others, being patient, loving others, etc. Let the children draw a pretty fruit or write a positive action on the healthy tree when they perform one of these fruits of the spirit.

  o At the end of the week, examine the tree and praise your child for his/her good fruit.

- Plant a garden of edible plants that can be grown in your area. Let your child enjoy the miracle of the full life cycle of a plant, including eating the fruit.

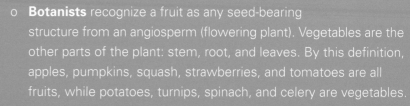

GO BEYOND

- Study the difference in a fruit and a vegetable:

  o **Botanists** recognize a fruit as any seed-bearing structure from an angiosperm (flowering plant). Vegetables are the other parts of the plant: stem, root, and leaves. By this definition, apples, pumpkins, squash, strawberries, and tomatoes are all fruits, while potatoes, turnips, spinach, and celery are vegetables.

  o **Chefs**, however, think in of terms of savory vegetables and sweet fruits. Botanical fruits such as bell peppers and tomatoes are vegetables by a chef's definition.

  o Further research: 1893 U.S. Supreme Court case *Nix v. Hedden*. Is a tomato a fruit of vegetable?

- Study the life and research of George Washington Carver.

PARTS OF A PLANT

SYMBIOSIS

Objectives: Define and understand symbiosis. Explore multiple examples of symbiotic relationships.

MATERIALS

1. Old magazines
2. Scissors
3. Glue
4. Blank index cards or folding cards
5. A few decorations for greeting cards (glitter, ribbon, stickers, or whatever you have on hand)

What are some living things?
(cats, dogs, people, plants, fish, worms, etc.)

BIG IDEA

When God created the Garden of Eden, He made all living things to live together in peace (Genesis 1 and 2). However, our perfect world was broken when Adam and Eve sinned. Now, all living things do not live together in peace (Genesis 3). It is a miracle that God left us with some wonderful examples of how He created things to exist

Symbiosis occurs when organisms (living things) live very closely together and depend on each other to thrive. If one is healthy, the other will probably be healthy too. If one moves, the other goes with it. Sometimes, if one dies, the other dies too.

Note to parents: This is mutualistic symbiosis, a lifelong relationship between different species in which they both benefit from their interaction.

Discuss how these familiar examples are representative of symbiosis:
- A milk cow and a farmer (The farmer gives the cow a barn, food, safety. The cow gives the farmer milk.)
- A clown fish and an anemone (The anemone gives the clown fish a safe home. The clown fish gives the anemone food.)
- A squirrel and an oak tree (the oak tree gives the squirrel food and a place to live. The squirrel buries acorns to plant more trees.)
- A Seeing Eye dog and a blind person (The person gives the dog food, shelter, and love. The dog gives the blind person companionship and help finding their way.)

SYMBIOSIS

 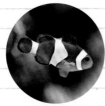  

BIG IDEA CONTINUED...

Can you think of any other examples of symbiosis?

The apostle, John, wrote a letter that tells us how we are to interact with each other. Just like some organisms have symbiosis to benefit each other, we are to love to benefit each other.

2 John 1:5-6, "And now, dear lady, I am not writing you a new command but one we have had from the beginning. I ask that we love one another. And this is love: that we walk in obedience to his commands. As you have heard from the beginning, *his command is that you walk in love.*

What does "walk in love" mean?

How can you show people you love them? Hugs, gifts, kind words, sharing, spending time, doing nice things, etc. God wants us to love each other.

LOVE NOTES:

ACTIVITY 1

1. Is there someone you love? Does anyone you know need some extra love?

2. We are going to make a card for that person in obedience with God's command to love.

3. Cut out pretty and cheerful pictures from the old magazines. Look especially for pictures of two living things benefiting each other.

   Ask children how the pictures they find are examples of symbiosis.

4. Cut out the letters "L" "O" "V" and "E" from the magazine or "F" "R" "I" "E" "N" "D".

5. Glue the pictures and letters in a collage on the index card or folding card.

6. Older children can write 2 John 1:5-6 on the back. Inspired children may make multiple cards. Remind them to keep the person who needs love in mind while they are creating the card.

SYMBIOSIS

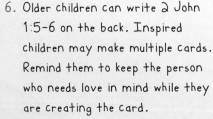

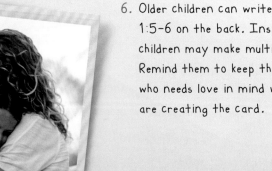

MATCHING HINTS:

Read the hints to the children.

Ask them to identify the symbiotic partners from the pictures below.

Hint	Partner 1	Partner 2	Symbiotic partners	
1	My home is very safe, because it will sting everyone except me.	I eat the leftovers from a funny fish.	Clown fish and Sea Anemone	
2	Some may think I swim in a dangerous place, but I love the leftovers. Plus, I get a free ride.	I don't mind the hitch hikers. They keep me clean.	Remora and Shark	
3	I love to lay my eggs on a special plant. My larvae babies need the seeds. I am very camouflaged in my home.	I need a very special pollinator to help me make seeds.	Yucca Moths and Yucca Flowers	
4	I know the way to the bee hive, but I am not strong enough to open it up. I love honey.	I have big claws to tear open a bee hive. However, I am too short to see where the hive is.	Honey Guide Bird and Honey Badger	
5	I need a safe place to live, and I love to eat ticks. I chirp if I see danger.	I need ticks removed, and my eyesight is poor. It is good to have an alarm if danger is near.	Oxpecker and Rhinoceros	
6	I need a good dentist to keep my teeth clean.	This may look like a dangerous place to eat, but it is safe for me.	Crocodile and Egyptian Plover	
7	I need to drink delicious nectar to keep me fluttering.	I love to be pollinated to make more seeds.	Butterfly and Flower	
8	My mouth is shaped like tweezers to pick food from between the sharp teeth of fish.	I go to the cleaning station as often as I like. It keeps me healthy.	Wrasse Cleaner and Eel	

NATURE WALK:

Go outside and look for examples of symbiosis. Here are a few you may find:

- Lichens on a rock. Although it looks like one organism, a lichen is actually algae and fungus growing together. The algae does photosynthesis to make food while the fungus absorbs water. "Alice Algae took a Lichen to Freddy Fungus, and their marriage has been on the rocks ever since."

- Insect pollinating a flower. The flower provides the insect with food (nectar and sometimes pollen). While the insect is busy probing for a meal, it doesn't realize that it is moving pollen from stamen to pistol, which is necessary for the flower to make seeds.

- Animals breathing while plants photosynthesize. The animals use oxygen and make carbon dioxide while the plants use carbon dioxide and make oxygen.

- Ants on a tree. The tree gives the ants a place to live while the ants protect the tree from insects that will eat its leaves.

- A squirrel burying an acorn. The squirrel will have food in the winter if it remembers where the acorn is buried. If it forgets, a new oak tree will grow.

APPLY IT

- Have the children draw or paint a picture of the two organisms in their favorite example of symbiosis (for instance: a butterfly and a flower).

- Search for more examples of mutualistic symbiosis in nature. Repeat 2 John 1:5-6 whenever you notice symbiosis.

- Study the story of Ruth and Naomi from the Book of Ruth. In verse 1:16-17 says, "But Ruth replied, "Don't urge me to leave you or to turn back from you. Where you go I will go, and where you stay I will stay. Your people will be my people and your God my God. Where you die I will die, and there I will be buried. May the Lord deal with me, be it ever so severely, if even death separates you and me."

  o Discuss how much Ruth loved Naomi.

  o How is this like mutualistic symbiosis, a lifelong relationship in which both organisms benefit from their interaction?

GO BEYOND

- Read the following verses to study how Christians are to treat one another. How is this like mutualistic symbiosis?

  o John 13:14 & 34
  o Romans 12:16, 14:13, & 15:7
  o 1 Corinthians 1:10
  o Galatians 5:15 & 6:2
  o Colossians 3:13
  o 1 Thessalonians 5:11 & 15
  o Hebrews 10:25
  o 1 Peter 3:8 & 4:8

- Explore the differences and similarities in the following various types of biological interactions:

  o Mutualistic symbiosis – both organisms benefit

  o Commensalistic symbiosis – the symbiont benefits with little effect on the host

  o Parasitic symbiosis – the symbiont benefits while the host is harmed

Further Reading:

How to Clean a Hippopotamus: A Look at Unusual Animal Partnerships by Robin Page and Steve Jenkins

Big Friend, Little Friend: A Book About Symbiosis by Susan Sussman and Robert James

Experiment 17:

BIRD POPULATION STUDY

Objective: Identify several local bird species. Understand the concept of a population study and data collection. Create a bar graph to represent data.

When God created this amazing planet, the land and the sea were complete, and beautiful plants grew everywhere. Do you remember what God did next?

Genesis 1:20-23.

And God said, "Let the water teem with living creatures, and let birds fly above the earth across the vault of the sky." So God created the great creatures of the sea and every living thing with which the water teems and that moves about in it, according to their kinds, and every winged bird according to its kind. And God saw that it was good. God blessed them and said, "Be fruitful and increase in number and fill the water in the seas, and let the birds increase on the earth." And there was evening, and there was morning – the fifth day.

BIG IDEA

MATERIALS

1. One dry pine cone per child
2. Peanut butter
3. Bird seed
4. A butter knife
5. One pipe cleaner per child
6. A book or website to identify local birds
7. Binoculars (optional)
8. Graph paper (optional)
9. One empty toilet paper roll per child
10. Scraps of construction paper or felt
11. An additional pipe cleaner cut into 1 inch lengths
12. Glue
13. Plastic googly eyes (optional)
14. Feathers (optional)

Today we are going to study God's birds.

Tell me about some birds you have seen. What colors are they? How big are they? Can they fly? What do they eat? Where do they live? Big birds, little birds, brown birds, red birds, cold weather birds, warm weather birds, etc. What is your favorite bird? What kind of birds do you see around your house?

BIRD POPULATION

BUILD A BIRD FEEDER:

ACTIVITY 1

1. Attach the pipe cleaner to the top of the pine cone. Remind children to be careful of the sharp points.

2. Use a butter knife to spread peanut butter all over pinecone. Press it into every crack to fully coat the pine cone. (In case of a peanut allergy, substitute with vegetable shortening.)

   a. Peanut butter is full of fat and protein, which are important for birds, especially in the winter.

3. Roll the peanut butter covered pine cone in a pile of bird seed until it is completely covered.

4. Hang your bird feeder so that you can see it from a window. Make sure it is not too low to tempt dogs.

5. It may take a day or two for the birds to find the feeder. Continue to Activity 3 and 4 when you notice that the birds are regularly visiting the feeder.

   a. Note: Birds benefit your yard by decreasing insect populations, eating weed seeds, and pollinating. See the previous lesson on symbiosis

BIRD CRAFT:
"MORE VALUABLE THAN THEY":

ACTIVITY 2

Matthew 6:26 - **Look** at the birds of the air; they do **not sow or reap or store away** in barns, and yet your heavenly Father feeds them. Are you **not** much **more valuable than they?**

   a. What do think this means? We are so valuable to God; He is our creator and provider. God does not want us to worry about anything in life. He loves us so much, even more than he loves the birds of the air.

   b. We are going to make a craft bird to remind you how valuable you are to God.

2. If you would like to create an owl, fold the top of the toilet paper roll down toward the middle, so "ears" stick up. If you would like to create a song bird, glue feathers on the top of the toilet paper roll.

3. Cut up the scraps of paper or felt to create a beak and wings. Glue the shaped scrap paper or felt appropriately to decorate the cardboard.

4. Attach googly eyes or draw eyes with a marker. Create legs with the 1 inch lengths of pipe cleaners.

5. Older children can write "much more valuable than they" on the back of the bird.

BIRD POPULATION

6. Every time you notice your bird, remember how valuable you are to God.

BIRD COUNT:

1. Find a place to sit still and quiet within sight of the bird feeder. An established, traditional bird feeder can substitute for the pine cone feeders. Birds are most active in the morning, for the two to three hours following sunrise.

2. When a bird is spotted, identify it and record it.

   a. Depending on the age of your students, you may choose to simply categorize birds by color or size. More advanced students may be able to truly identify various species.

   b. Tally marks are a preferable means of record keeping if your students are able. Otherwise, a simple mark for each bird is fine. Younger students can use colors to create categories for various birds. For instance, draw a red box and ask the child to put one red dot in the red box for each red bird he sees.

3. Continue to identify and count birds until attention spans wane.

ACTIVITY 3

BAR GRAPH:

ACTIVITY 4

1. Create a bar graph to represent the bird count.

2. The horizontal (x) axis lists the various birds. The vertical (y) axis counts from zero up to at least the highest number of birds recorded.

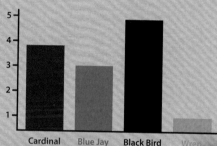

Cardinal   Blue Jay   Black Bird   Wren

APPLY IT

- Genesis 2:15 says, "The Lord God took the man and put him in the Garden of Eden to work it and take care of it." God called Adam to take care of the Garden. And it is our responsibility to take care of the earth now. How can you help take care of the earth? Are you being a good caretaker by feeding the birds?

- Continue to identify local birds while you go about your day. Teach your child to identify 3 or 4 of the most common birds in your area.

- Build a feather collection.

- Study the life of Jack Miner, an amazing bird conservationist.

GO BEYOND

- Study the songs and sounds of your local birds. Repeat the population study by using ears instead of eyes.

- Choose a few of the local bird species to study further: diet, migration routes, reproduction, behavior, etc. Add a bird bath, a bird house, and species specific bird feeders to your yard.

- Discuss the meaning of the following quote from Martin Luther. "No one can calculate God's care of animals in nature. I am sure God's expenditure, just for sparrows, comes to more than the annual revenue of the King of France."

ENDOSKELETON VERSUS EXOSKELETON

Objectives: Define endoskeleton and exoskeleton. Identify organisms with endoskeleton, exoskeleton, and no skeleton.

MATERIALS

1. 4 x 6 note cards or 11 x 13 cardstock cut in half (2 per child)

2. Old printed media (magazines

3. Newspapers, calendars, etc.)

4. Scissors

5. Glue sticks

6. Play Dough

Why did God give you bones? (To help you stand up and move). Did God give all creatures bones? Can you think of any creatures that do not have bones? (Worms, snails, crabs, etc.)

Your bones make up your skeletal system. Your skeleton is inside your body; this is an **endoskeleton**. "Endo" means inside; an endoskeleton is an inside skeleton. Insects and crustaceans have hard shells on the outside of their bodies; this is an **exoskeleton**. "Exo" means outside; an exoskeleton is an outside skeleton. Some creatures don't have any skeleton at all, like worms, octopuses, and jelly fish. These are called **soft bodied organisms**.

Note: Of the approximately 40 phyla in the animal kingdom, only Chordata possess complex endoskeletons. Phyla Echinodermata, Porifera, and subclass Coleoida have primitive endoskeletons. All other organisms in the animal kingdom either possess exoskeletons or are soft bodied.

BIG IDEA

SEARCH FOR CREATURES:

ACTIVITY 1

1. Ask the children to write "endoskeleton" on one card and "exoskeleton" on the other card.

2. Give each child a magazine, ask them to find any animals with an endoskeleton or an exoskeleton. It is unlikely that the children will find pictures of soft bodied organisms, but if they do, make a card for "soft bodied" as well.

3. Then glue the cut out animals to the correct card; use front and back of the card. Allow the children to label and glue more cards if they wish.

4. The cards can be studied and added to for weeks.

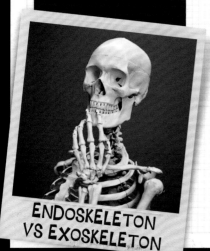

ENDOSKELETON VS EXOSKELETON

God's Creatures:

1. Read the following day six story of creation from Genesis 1:24: God said, "Let the land produce living creatures according to their kinds: the livestock, the creatures that move along the ground, and the wild animals, each according to its kind." And it was so. God made the wild animals according to their kinds, the livestock according to their kinds, and all the creatures that move along the ground according their kinds. And God saw that it was good.

> Psalm 104:24 says, "How many are your works, Lord! In wisdom you made them all; the earth is full of your creatures."

2. God made ALL of the creatures, even the ones we think are slimy or squirmy. He created them all for His reasons.

3. Ask the children to quietly think of their favorite creature with an exoskeleton and their favorite creature with an endoskeleton. Don't say the creatures out loud.

4. Give each child a tub of play dough. Instruct them to form the two creatures: one with an exoskeleton and one with an endoskeleton. But do not tell anyone which creatures they formed.

5. Note: How realistic the creature looks is not as important as the act of creating something from clay.

6. Ask each child to hold his/her animals up one at a time while the other kids guess. Make sure the type of skeleton is mentioned for each animal. Allow children to share why they like these animals.

7. After all have shared, remind them that they have created a creature from clay. It was shapeless before they started, and they formed it with their hands. This is similar to how God formed the living creatures, but God made them perfect. Are your creatures perfect? God breathed life into them? Are your creatures alive?

Nature Walk:

Go for a walk in a park or wooded area. Look for animals with various types of skeletons:
- Endoskeletons: dog, squirrel, bird, lizard, fish, etc.
- Exoskeletons: dragonfly, mosquito, snail, etc.
- Soft bodied organisms: worms.

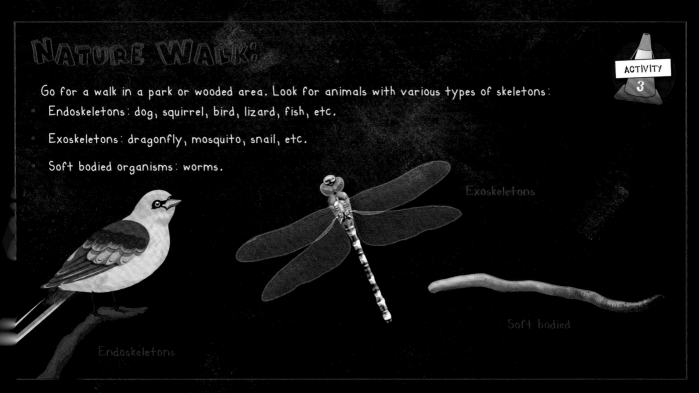

Exoskeletons

Soft bodied

Endoskeletons

- As you go through your week, point out animals with endoskeletons and animals with exoskeletons. Use these animals as reminders to review Psalm 104:24.

- Play charades. One person stands in front of the room. That person will whisper to the teacher which living creature they will act out, and whether it has an exoskeleton or an endoskeleton.

Then the child will act out their creature without using their voice. The rest of the children should guess what creature the child is acting out. Whoever guesses correctly is the next person to act out an animal.

APPLY IT

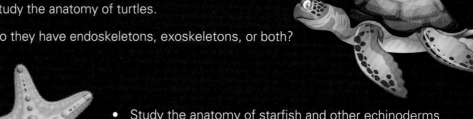

- Study the anatomy of turtles.

  Do they have endoskeletons, exoskeletons, or both?

- Study the anatomy of starfish and other echinoderms (sea urchins, sea cucumber, and brittle stars).

  Do they have endoskeletons, exoskeletons, both, or neither?

MORE SCIENCE

Chitin is the main component of exoskeletons. French chemist, Henri Braconnot, discovered it in 1811 by isolating it from mushrooms. It is a very common in nature, being found in both exoskeletons and many fungi cell walls. Chitin gives exoskeletal animals many benefits; it is very light-weight, tough, and water proof. However, it must be shed as the animal grows, and it is only flexible at the joints. Scientists are currently learning new uses for chitin. It has been discovered to have anti-inflammatory benefits, be anti-bacterial, stimulate the immune system, and act as an anti-cancer agent.

Reference: Applications of Chitin and Its Derivatives in Biological Medicine

Bae Keun Park, Moon-Moo Kim

Int J Mol Sci. 2010; 11(12): 5152-5164. Published online 2010 December 15. doi: 10.3390/ijms11125152. PMCID: PMC3100826

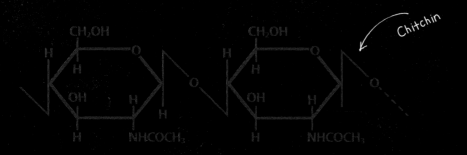

Chitchin

ENDOSKELETON VS EXOSKELETON

Experiment 19:

CARNIVORES, HERBIVORES, & OMNIVORES: THE FOOD CHAIN

Objectives: Define carnivore, herbivore, and omnivore. Understand the anatomical differences between carnivores, herbivores, and omnivores. Construct food chains and a food web to understand the flow of energy through an ecosystem.

MATERIALS

1. Picture of a horse or deer with face visible
2. Picture of wolf or tiger with face visible
3. Either one large mirror or a small hand mirror for each child
4. At least 8 sheets of blank paper
5. Markers or crayons
6. A ball of yarn or string
7. Tape
8. Scissors

God created all different kinds of creatures to eat all different kinds of food. What is your favorite food?

BIG IDEA

Originally, the Bible tells us that God made a perfect world in which all creatures ate plants:

"And to all the beasts of the earth and all the birds in the sky and all the creatures that move along the ground - everything that has the breath of life in it - I give every green plant for food." And it was so." Genesis 1:30

But because of sin, death came into the world, and it was not perfect any more. Now, many creatures eat each other. But one day Jesus will return this earth to its perfect state. Then everything and everyone will live in perfect peace!

Can you imagine a world with perfect peace?
Allow children to brainstorm answers.

THE FOOD CHAIN

BIG IDEA CONTINUED... Read Isaiah 65:17-25 for a beautiful description of our future with the Lord in the New Heavens and New Earth.

"See, I will create
  new heavens and a new earth.
The former things will not be remembered,
  nor will they come to mind.
But be glad and rejoice forever
  in what I will create,
for I will create Jerusalem to be a delight
  and its people a joy.
I will rejoice over Jerusalem
  and take delight in my people;
the sound of weeping and of crying
  will be heard in it no more.

"Never again will there be in it
  an infant who lives but a few days,
  or an old man who does not live out his years;
the one who dies at a hundred
  will be thought a mere child;
the one who fails to reach a hundred
  will be considered accursed.
They will build houses and dwell in them;
  they will plant vineyards and eat their fruit.
No longer will they build houses and others live in them,
  or plant and others eat.
For as the days of a tree,
  so will be the days of my people;
my chosen ones will long enjoy
  the work of their hands.
They will not labor in vain,
  nor will they bear children doomed to misfortune;
for they will be a people blessed by the LORD,
  they and their descendants with them.
Before they call I will answer;
  while they are still speaking I will hear.

The wolf and the lamb will feed together, and the lion will eat straw like the ox, and dust will be the serpent's food. They will neither harm nor destroy on all my holy mountain," says the Lord.

Can you imagine a wolf grazing on clover next to a lamb? Or a lion munching on straw with an ox. Or a snake eating dust? It's pretty difficult to picture. That time is yet to come. Today we are going to discuss the diets of creatures living in our current world:

- What are some animals that eat only plants? (cows, horses, deer, rabbit) These animals are called herbivores. In nature, they are often prey animals, hunted and eaten by other animals.
- What are some animals that eat only meat? (tiger, wolf, dolphin, crocodiles). These animals are called carnivores. In nature, they are called predators because they hunt and eat prey.
- What are some animals that eat both plants and meat? (humans, bears, raccoons, opossums, ducks, turtles). These animals are called omnivores.

God equipped each animal with the tools it needs to eat.

THE FOOD CHAIN

COMPARE AND CONTRAST:

THE FOOD CHAIN

Herbivore

1. Place the picture of the horse or deer in front of the students.
   What do you notice about this animal?

   a. Legs: Do you see its long legs? Why did God give it long legs? To outrun a predator.

   b. Eyes: Do you see that its eyes are on the sides of its head? Why did God place its eyes on the sides of its head? To see predators sneaking up on it from any direction.

   c. Teeth: Feel the teeth in the back of your mouth. These are your **molars**. You use your molars to grind up food. Herbivores like deer and horses have great molars for grinding up all those grasses and leaves.

   d. Digestion: Herbivores have very long digestive systems. Some even have four stomachs! It takes a long time to get nutrients out of plants.

Carnivore

2. Place the picture of the wolf or tiger in front of the students. What do you notice about this animal?

   a. Eyes: Do you see that its eyes are on the front of its head? Why did God place its eyes on the front of its head? To use both eyes to catch prey. Binocular vision allows an animal to have depth perception.

      i. Hold up your finger and ask a student to touch your finger. Then ask him to cover one eye and touch your finger. Was it harder to judge depth? Binocular vision is very important for a predator leaping at or chasing prey.

   b. Teeth: Feel the sharp teeth in the sides of the front of your mouth. These are your **canines**. You use your canines to tear meat. Carnivores like wolves and tiger have great canines for tearing up the meat of the prey animals they kill and eat.

   c. Claws: If you are using a tiger picture, point out the use of claws in catching and killing prey.

   d. Digestion: Carnivores have short digestive systems. The meat passes through quickly so it does not rot.

Omnivore

3. Look in the mirror. What do you notice about yourself?

   a. Eyes: Where are your eyes? They are on the front of your face. This allows people to be excellent hunters.

   b. Teeth: What kind of teeth do you have? You have Incisors for crunching veggies, canines for tearing meat, and molars for grinding food.

   c. Hand: Look at your hand? Does it have claws for catching a deer? Or is it better suited for picking an apple?

   d. Digestion: Do you think raw chicken looks or smells yummy? What about fried chicken, is it yummy? People cannot digest raw meat. God gave us a strong instinct to reject uncooked meat. But we can digest cooked meat. Yet our small intestine is very long like an herbivore, ideal for digesting vegetables.

   It is great to be an omnivore because they have SO many choices of food.

4. Have more advanced students create 3 lists to describe the characteristics of herbivores, carnivores, and omnivores.

FOOD CHAIN:

All living things need a source of energy. This energy helps animals and people move and grow. Even plants need energy to grow and bloom. From where does this energy come? From where do you get all of your energy? Food. What have you eaten today? Have you eaten like an herbivore, carnivore, or omnivore?

Plants use photosynthesis to make their own food from the energy of the sun's light combined with carbon dioxide from the air and water from the soil. Where do the herbivores get energy? They eat the plants. Where do the carnivores get energy? They eat other animals. For example, through photosynthesis an apple tree uses the sun's energy to make sugars in its leaves. The tree relocates the sugars from the leaves to the tip of a twig to grow an apple. Then along comes a hungry deer. The deer eats the apple for energy. Then along comes a hungry wolf. The wolf kills the deer and eats it for energy. A **food chain** is a transfer of energy. The energy moves from one living thing to another. The arrows show where the energy moves.

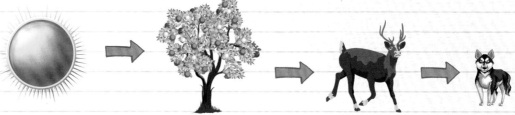

All living creatures ultimately depend on green plants for food. How does the wolf depend on the apple tree?

1. Ask children to trace the flow of energy through the following organisms:

2. The sun shines on the grass. The grass does photosynthesis, making sugars. The grass hopper, the herbivore, eats the grass. The western meadow lark, the omnivore, eats the grasshopper.

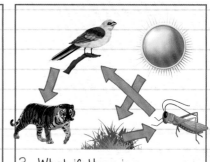

3. What if there is a big carnivore?

   What if a bobcat is in this ecosystem?

4. The bobcat would probably eat the meadow lark. That would be the end of the food chain, unless another carnivore ate the bobcat.

5. Ask children to construct their own food chain. Guide them to begin by drawing a sun, then draw a plant, then draw an herbivore, then draw a carnivore that would eat that herbivore. Remember, arrows show direction of flow of energy.

THE FOOD CHAIN

FOOD WEB:

ACTIVITY 3

1. If there are 8 or more children in the class, assign each child one of the following pictures to draw and color on the blank paper. If there are more than 16 children, add to the list if necessary, keeping a relatively even distribution of plants, herbivores, omnivores, and carnivores. If there are fewer than 8 children, assign older children two pictures to draw. Be sure to assign at least 2 items from each category. The teacher draws the sun.

	Plants	Herbivores	Carnivores	Omnivores
Sun	Clover	Rabbit	Snake	Hawk
	Grass	Caterpillar	Spider	Wolf
	Apple	Grasshopper	Frog	Mountain lion
	Flower	Mouse	Racoon	

2. Have the children tape the pictures to the floor in a circle, with the sun in the center. Ask children to sit down behind their picture(s).

3. The teacher/sun begins with the ball of yarn in the center of the circle. The ball of yarn represents the sun's energy. Tape the loose end of the yarn to the sun, then roll the ball of yarn to a "plant".
   - This is the first step in a food chain, the sun giving energy to a plant.

4. The student with the plant picture tapes the yarn to his/her plant drawing, then rolls the ball of yarn to an herbivore or an omnivore, any animal that would eat that plant.
   - This is the second step in a food chain, the plant giving energy to an herbivore or omnivore.

5. That student tapes the yarn to his/her herbivore drawing, then rolls the ball of yarn to a carnivore or omnivore, any animal that would eat the previous herbivore or omnivore.
   - Sometimes, a carnivore or omnivore is the end of that food chain because they are a top predator. Sometimes they are eaten by another carnivore or omnivore.

6. That student tapes the yarn to his/her carnivore or omnivore drawing, the rolls the ball of yarn to a bigger carnivore or omnivore, if there is one in the food web.

7. When the first food chain is complete, cut the yarn and tape the end to the final predator.
   - For instance, the sun shines on the grass, the caterpillar eats the grass, the spider eats the caterpillar, and the raccoon eats the spider.
   - This yarn shows the flow of energy from the sun all the way to the raccoon.

THE FOOD CHAIN

8. The teacher goes back to the sun in the center and begins the process again. Encourage children to choose various organisms as they roll the ball of yarn. However, if the same creature is chosen two or three times, it is fine.

9. Repeat the process until all organisms have been used at least once. Stand back and look at the beautiful food web! A **food web** is a complex network of food chains in an ecosystem.

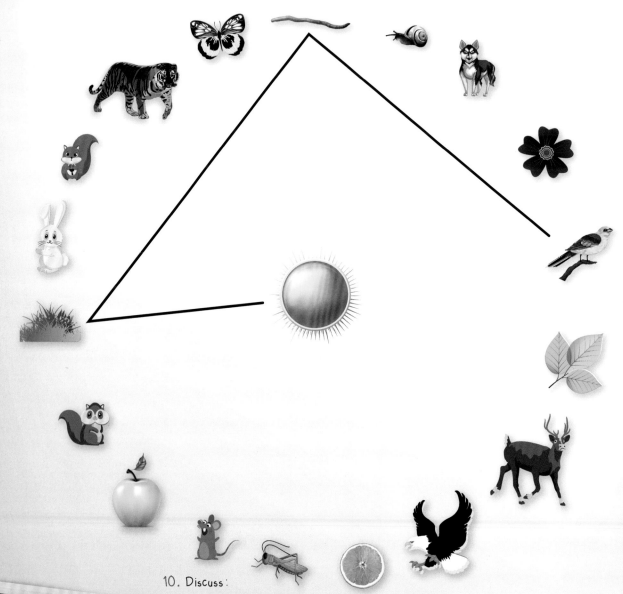

10. Discuss:

   • How many food chains did you make? Many.

   • How many food webs did you make? One, a food web is made up of many food chains.

   • Which picture has the most pieces of yarn? The sun.
     Why? Every green plant depends on the sun, and every animal depends on green plants, directly or indirectly.

   • Why is every creature important? Living things depend on each other. Choose one of the green plants, detach or cut the yarn from its picture. Which herbivores suffer? Which carnivores suffer when those herbivores suffer?

THE FOOD CHAIN

- Discuss the diet of any animals you see, domestic or wild. For example:
  - o Cows, goats, and horses are herbivores, feeding exclusively on grass and shrubs.
  - o Dogs and cats are carnivores, although some dogs will eat vegetables.
  - o Pigs and chickens are omnivores, eating insects, seeds, roots, even small reptiles and mammals.
  - o Many song birds are omnivores, feeding on both insects and seeds. Hawks and eagles are carnivores.
  - o Ducks and geese are omnivores, feeding on plant matter, small fish, and crustaceans.
  - o Most humans are omnivores, except for vegetarians and vegans.
  - o Bees and termites are herbivores. Bees drink nectar and pollen. Termites eat wood.
  - o Many lizards and turtles are omnivores, feeding on insects, worms, and plant matter.
- Study the return of Christ. Isaiah 11:6, Isaiah 65:25, Matthew 16:18, Colossians 1:13, Hebrews 12:28, John 11:25, Colossians 2:12, 3:1, Romans 6:3-5, and Revelation 6:9-11.
- Wouldn't it be awesome if you could just hold your arms out and turn your face toward the sun and do photosynthesis whenever you felt hungry?

- Discuss advantages and disadvantages of being herbivorous, carnivorous, or omnivorous.
- Study the definition and role of a keystone species.
  - o A keystone species is an animal (or occasionally a plant) that plays a vital role in an ecosystem. If the keystone species becomes extinct, the ecosystem will change dramatically. Very often, the keystone species is a big predator.
  - o For instance, consider the mountain lion. What does it eat? Deer, birds, rabbits. What would happen to the deer population if the mountain lion doesn't exist? The deer will have lots of babies but no predator to reduce the population. What will happen to the food and water supplies if there are too many deer in the ecosystem? There will not be enough food and water for all of the animals and the whole ecosystem will suffer. See how important the keystone mountain lion is?
- Draw a food web for the ecosystem in which you live.
- Read and discuss the meanings of Genesis 9:3, Romans 14:1-23, and Isaiah 11:6.
- Consider the benefits to the food web when wolves were reintroduced to Yellowstone.
- Pandas are fond of only one food source. Why is this detrimental?

How the Moon Shines

Objectives: Understand that the moon reflects light from the sun.

MATERIALS

1. A room that can be completely darkened

2. A volleyball sized white ball or balloon hanging near the ceiling

3. A good flashlight

4. Several large stuffed animals (1 per child plus a few extras)

5. One white poster board

Genesis 1:16 tells us that **"God made two great lights—the greater light to govern the day and the lesser light to govern the night."**

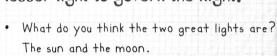

- What do you think the two great lights are? The sun and the moon.

- Why did God make the sun? Light in the day, energy, photosynthesis.

- Why did God make the moon? Light at night, keep calendar, tides.

BIG IDEA

Lunar Reflection:

ACTIVITY 1

1. Did you know that the moon actually reflects the light from the sun (like a mirror reflects your face)? The sun creates light and shines brightly, but the moon simply reflects the light from the sun to shine on the darkened earth.

2. Explain that the flashlight represents the sun. Does the flashlight shine? Does it make its own light? (yes)

3. Explain that the ball/balloon represents the moon. Does the ball/balloon shine? Does it make its own light? (no) Then let's explore how God causes the moon to shine!

4. Hang the ball near the ceiling, a few feet away.

5. With the flashlight off, darken the room. Is the ball bright? No.

6. Turn on the flashlight, and point it upward toward the ball. Is the flashlight shining?

7. Is the ball bright? Does it appear to be shining in the darkness?

8. Turn the flashlight back off. Is the ball bright?

9. The ball is not bright when the flashlight is off because it has no source of light to reflect.

10. The moon appears to shine because it reflects light from the sun.

HOW THE MOON SHINES

LUNAR REFLECTION LOST-AND-FOUND:

ACTIVITY
2

NAME	STUFFED ANIMAL
Betty	Big, brown bear with the blue tie

1. Before the activity, make a list of the children's names and list a specific stuffed animal beside each child's name. For instance: "Betty – big, brown bear with the blue tie." You will need to be somewhat familiar with this list or have a small pin light with which to read it in the dark.

2. Place the stuffed animals around the room. Push obstructions, such as furniture, against the wall or out of the room.

3. Instruct children to sit on the floor in the center of the room. Tell them to study the positions of the various stuffed animals.

4. Turn off the lights so the room is completely dark.

5. Call a child's name. Ask him/her to crawl around the room to find a specific stuffed animal, and return to his/her seat.

6. Take turns calling each child's name and asking him/her to find a specific stuffed animal until all children have had a turn.

7. Turn the lights on. Reread the list. Who found the correct stuffed animal? Who found their stuffed animal with ease? Who found it difficult or impossible?

8. Place the stuffed animals around the room again.

9. Instruct children to sit back in the center of the room. Repeat steps 4-6 while you shine the flashlight up at the white ball.

10. Now who found the correct stuffed animal? Was it easier with a light?

11. Can you imagine how dark it would be if God had not created light to help us at night? It is easy to get lost and confused on a dark night. The light of the moon helps us find our way.

LIGHT OF THE WORLD, REFLECTING JESUS'S LIGHT:

ACTIVITY
3

In John 8:12 "When Jesus spoke again to the people, he said, "I am the light of the world. Whoever follows me will never walk in darkness, but will have the light of life."

Continued on the next page

1. Jesus's light is like the sun, burning brightly to give light. Jesus came into this world to save us from the darkness. If you are lost or scared, Jesus is your help. If you do not have Jesus, it is impossible to find your way through the darkness.

2. If Jesus is the light of the world, what are we?

3. In Matthew 5:14 – 15, Jesus says, "You are the light of the world. A town built on a hill cannot be hidden. Neither do people light a lamp and put it under a bowl. Instead they put it on its stand, and it gives light to everyone in the house."

4. Before we become Christians, we are in spiritual darkness. When we accept Christ, we step into His light. Like the moon reflects the light of the sun, to light the darkened earth. So we are supposed to reflect the light of Jesus to light the darkened earth. How can you be the light of the world? How can you reflect Jesus's love?

5. While children brainstorm answers to this question, cut out a large circle from the poster board. This represents the moon.

6. Allow children to write or draw their ideas about reflecting Jesus's love on the poster board. A few ideas may include: talk about Jesus when you are with friends, do not be ashamed of your testimony, pray over meals at school and restaurants, ask friends to pray with you, let others know how much you love Jesus, help others, love people who are difficult to love, exhibit the fruits of the spirit (love, joy, peace, forbearance, kindness, goodness, faithfulness, gentleness and self-control), and live life for God.

7. Display the poster board for a few days. Add to it when you notice a student acting in a Christ like way.

- Observe the moon in any phase; remind children how God created the sun, moon, and stars. Remember that the moon reflects the sun's light in order to give light to the night. Use binoculars or a telescope to observe the details of the moon.

- Where else do you see light reflected to make things appear to shine? Observe the reflection of car headlights on street signs, birthday candles illuminating a person's face before he blows them out, a light shining in a mirror, any toys with glitter and shine.

APPLY IT

- Sing "This Little Light of Mine"

- Study the references to light in the following verses. Ask children to explain what each verse means. Discuss how they can apply each verse.

  - Psalm 18:28
  - Psalm 119:105
  - Isaiah 50:10
  - Isaiah 60:19
  - Micah 7:9
  - Matthew 5:16
  - Matthew 6:22
  - John 1:3-5
  - John 3:18-20
  - Romans 13:12

HOW THE MOON SHINES

- The sun converts about 600 million tons of hydrogen in to helium every second. This releases an enormous amount of energy that leaves the sun in all directions. Some of the energy from the sun falls on the planets and moons in our solar system. Different objects have different abilities to reflect. **Albedo** is the word astronomers use to refer to the amount of reflected light. The numerical value for albedo ranges from 0 (dark) to 1 (bright). The moon's albedo is 0.12, or the moon reflects 12% of the sunlight that hits it. One of Saturn's moons, Enceladus, has the highest albedo in our solar system (0.99) because it is covered in ice. The asteroids between Mars and Jupiter have about the lowest albedo in our solar system (0.05) because they are a dull dark color.

  GO BEYOND

  o Conduct an experiment to observe the albedos of various surfaces. Use your imagination to think of several materials with different albedos. Wrap tennis balls in these various materials and shine a light on them in a darkened room. The color of the surface of the moon is a light gray.

  o Although the moon only reflects 12% of the light that hits it, when it is full it lights up the night when it is full. A full-moon night is bright enough to walk around comfortably and almost read. This is because of how amazingly bright our sun shines. This is an excellent example of how Jesus loves us. His love is so great; His light is so bright. If we can reflect just a bit of it back into the darkened world, it will provide light. Not because of our ability to reflect, but because of His ability to shine.

Starry Night Art Project

ACTIVITY

MATERIALS

1. Paper (white construction paper, cardstock, or watercolor paper)
3. White and yellow crayons
4. Watercolor paint (black, blue, and purple)

1. Examine "Starry Night", the painting by Vincent Van Gogh. Can you see the moon? Can you see the stars? What else do you see in the painting?

2. Give each student a sheet of white cardstock or construction paper and yellow and white crayons.

3. Ask them to draw and color a moon and stars with the crayons. Press firmly when coloring.

4. When the drawing is complete, ask students to brush black, blue, and purple watercolor paint all over their drawings. The crayon wax will repel the water based paint, so the stars and moon shine through the darkness!

HOW THE MOON SHINES

Experiment 21:

WEATHERING & EROSION

Objectives: Define and explore mechanical weathering, chemical weathering, and erosion. Explore the effects of weathering and erosion.

MATERIALS

1. Sugar cubes (one or two per child)
2. A clear plastic cup
3. A freezer
4. Two pieces of chalk
5. 1 cup vinegar
6. 1 cup water
7. Two 9"x13" dishes
8. 5 cups of sand
9. 5 cups rocks or pebbles
10. Plenty of water
11. A measuring cup
13. Dry sand or dirt
14. Hair dryer
15. Two small model houses (two wooden blocks can substitute)

[SAFETY NOTE: Wear safety glasses when using the hairdryer to move sand. Make sure to point the hairdryer away from other people. Most of these activities are best done outside.]

BIG IDEA

Have you ever had a difficult time? Ask children if they would like to share some of their difficult experiences.

Once, there was a man named Job. He had a very difficult time. He lost his herds, servants, home, children, noble reputation, and good health. But even in his despair, he did not lose his faith in God. He understood God's power to give blessings and to take them away. Job compared God's power to weathering and erosion. Job 14:18-19 states, "But as a mountain erodes and crumbles and as a rock is moved from its place, as water wears away stones and torrents wash away the soil, so [God] destroys a person's hope."

Weathering and erosion are destructive forces. They break down and move rocks. Over time, they change entire landscapes. Something must be quite powerful to break down and move rocks. It's no wonder that Job compared God's power to weathering and erosion. Everything in his life was broken down and taken away.

What are some forces in the world that might break down rocks? (wind, water, waves, rivers, ice, car tires, bull dozers, shoes, hammers, etc.) These are all examples of **mechanical weathering**. Mechanical weathering occurs when rocks are simply broken into smaller pieces.

Chemical weathering occurs when rocks are changed because they are exposed to chemicals that actually change them into a different substance. This is like metal rusting and acidic water dissolving rock to form a cave.

Erosion occurs when rocks are moved by rivers, wind, and glaciers.

First, weathering breaks rocks into smaller pieces. Then, the pieces are easily eroded by water or wind.

MECHANICAL WEATHERING BY PRESSURE:

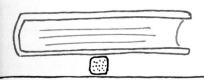

1. Give each student a sugar cube.
2. Ask them to break the sugar cube down using their body weight or a heavy book.

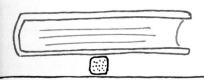

3. This is how many rocks are mechanically weathered on the surface of the earth. What are some forms of pressure rocks experience? (people and animals walking, cars driving, powerful waves crashing down, tectonic plates grinding together, glaciers flowing, and even plants roots growing into cracks of rocks can expand the cracks).

EATHERING & EROSION

MECHANICAL WEATHERING BY FREEZING EXPANSION:

1. Fill a clear plastic cup half way with water. Mark the exact line of the water on the outside of the cup.

2. Form a hypothesis: Does water change volume when it turns to ice?
3. Place it in a freezer until water freezes (about 1 hour).
4. Observe the line.
5. Water expands when it freezes. Most rocks have small cracks in them. If water makes its way inside the crack of a rock and then freezes, it will expand to enlarge the crack. When this happens many times, the rock will break. This is called an ice wedge and is a form of mechanical weathering.
   a. Ice wedges cause many of the potholes in the roads. Water runs into small cracks in the pavement, then freezes, expands, and widens the cracks. This process is repeated until the pavement breaks apart.

CHEMICAL WEATHERING BY ACID:

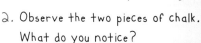

1. Place one piece of chalk (limestone) in a cup of water. Place one piece of chalk (limestone) in a cup of vinegar.
2. Observe the two pieces of chalk. What do you notice?
3. Form a hypothesis: Which chalk will dissolve first?

4. Observe the two pieces of chalk after one hour, and again after 24 hours.
5. The acid of the vinegar dissolves carbonate based rocks like chalk, limestone, and marble. Rain is naturally slightly acidic due to mixing with carbon dioxide in the air. Pollution creates acid rain that dissolves rocks more quickly than regular rainwater. This is a form of **chemical weathering**.

EROSION BY WIND:

1. Place dry sand or dirt in a Pyrex dish.

2. Use a hairdryer to move the particles around the dish.

3. Wind erodes tons of soil around the earth every year.

EROSION BY WATER, PARTICLE SIZE COMPARISON:

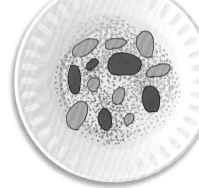

1. Read the story from Matthew 7:24 – 27.

Matthew 7:24, "Therefore everyone who hears these words of mine and puts them into practice is like a wise man who built his house on the rock.

The rain came down, the streams rose, and the winds blew and beat against that house; yet it did not fall, because it had its foundation on the rock. But everyone who hears these words of mine and does not put them into practice is like a foolish man who built his house on sand. The rain came down, the streams rose, and the winds blew and beat against that house, and it fell with a great crash."

2. Place the two Pyrex dishes side by side.

3. Fill the end of one of the dishes with sand. Fill the end of the other dish with pebbles/rocks. Push the particles up to one end of the dish, so the opposite end is empty.

4. Place one model house on each pile. If time allows, let children use sticks and leaves to create a landscape.

5. Form a hypothesis: If water is poured over each pile of particles, which one will erode more, the sand or the pebbles?

6. Test the hypothesis by pouring one cup of water over each of the piles to represent flood waters. Repeat two or three times.

7. Which one erodes more? Why?

8. Smaller particles are more easily washed away. This is erosion.

9. What is Jesus teaching us in the story of the wise and foolish builder?

   a. The wise man: People who listen to Jesus' words and obey build their lives on the solid foundation of faith and love. They will stand strong under pressure, just as the house on the rock stood firm.

   b. The foolish man: People who seem to listen and understand but do not obey, do not have a strong foundation when problems come. They will fall under the strain, just as the house on the sand washed away.

WEATHERING & EROSION

- Look for examples of weathering and erosion as you drive and walk. Construction sites, river banks, agricultural fields, muddy streams, etc.

- Take note of the destructive chemical weathering of marble statues.

- Job 42:12-17 resolves the story of Job. "The Lord blessed the latter part of Job's life more than the former part. He had fourteen thousand sheep, six thousand camels, a thousand yoke of oxen and a thousand donkeys. And he also had seven sons and three daughters. The first daughter he named Jemimah, the second Keziah, and the third Keren-Happuch. Nowhere in all the land were there found women as beautiful as Job's daughters, and their father granted them an inheritance along with their brothers. After this, Job lived a hundred and forty years; he saw his children and their children to the fourth generation. And so Job died, an old man and full of years."

  o Although the Lord took away Job's blessings when he was young, Job did not lose his faith. Thus, the Lord bountifully restored Job's blessings.

  o In nature, weathering breaks down rocks and erosion moves rocks. But deposition restores landscapes. Just as Job's blessings were taken away and later new blessings were bestowed, so the processes of weathering and erosion are restored by deposition.

  o **Deposition** is the means by which pieces of rock, sand, and dirt are laid down in a new place. This process creates many landforms. Wind deposits eroded sand to create sand dunes. Streams deposit eroded soil to create deltas. Ocean waves deposit sand and coral pieces to create beaches. The Nile River of Egypt was an excellent example of how weathering, erosion, and deposition can help people. Every year, the Nile flooded and deposited new soil over the land. This fertile land created bountiful crops for the Egyptian people, allowing their civilization to flourish.

- As your child makes decisions, mention the parable of the wise and foolish builders. For instance, if your child enjoys Sunday school class, tell your child that he/she is a wise builder by listening to and obeying God's instructions.

WEATHERING
& EROSION

- Help your student design and conduct an experiment to test how the root systems of plants influence erosion.

- Study the causes and effects of the Dust Bowl of the United States and Canada during the Great Depression of the 1930s.

- Help you student design and conduct an experiment to test how the size of cracks in rocks is increased by the freezing and expansion of water.

- Meticulously read the story from Matthew 7:24 – 27. What forms of erosion are mentioned? Repeat Activity 5, but invent ways to demonstrate the rain falling, the stream rising, and the wind blowing.

SINKHOLES & CHEMICAL WEATHERING

ACTIVITY

1. Give each child a plastic cup.

MATERIALS

1. Sugar cubes
2. Graham crackers
3. Vinegar
4. Dropper
5. Clear cup

2. Fill the bottom of the cup with one layer of sugar cubes. These represent a layer of bedrock. Lay a graham cracker piece on top of the sugar cubes to represent the soil.

3. Using the vinegar in the dropper, drop in onto the "soil" graham cracker. This is like rain seeping down into the ground. What happens over time?

4. The rock under the soil gives way, causing the soil to sink. This is how sinkholes form. They occur due to erosion of bedrock by water. Water is constantly seeping down into the ground. It slowly weathers and erodes rocks and minerals. Occasionally, the flow of water is so great that it washes away the underground structural bedrock. Salt deposits, limestone, and other carbonate rocks are most susceptible. These rocks become weakened long before there is visible evidence on the surface. When the structural bedrock becomes too weak to support the surface of the earth, it collapses and opens a sinkhole.

Bimmah sinkhole, Oman

ARCHIMEDES OF SYRACUS

Archimedes of Syracus was the foremost scientist of the classical age and has been called the most excellent scientist of all time. He was born on the tiny Greek island of Syracuse in about 287 BC. The Greeks were the first people to do science for the purpose of pursuing knowledge. Engrossed in the science of the Ancient Greeks, Archimedes intellect quickly expanded further than any of his predecessors or contemporaries.

Legend has it that King Hiero II hired a craftsman to make him a gold crown. The king gave the craftsman an amount of gold for the project. When the king received the finished product, he thought that the craftsman had stolen some of the gold and replaced it with less valuable silver. But how could he be sure? Archimedes solved the problem. Gold was known to be denser than silver. Density equals mass divided by volume. The mass of the crown was found by using a scale. To find the volume of the irregularly shaped crown, Archimedes lowered it into a cylinder of water and observed how much the water level increased. Archimedes discovered that the crown was a mixture of silver and gold. This was bad news for the king and the craftsman. The story goes that the solution to finding the volume of the crown occurred to Archimedes while he was taking a bath. He noticed how the water level in the tub rose when he got in. He was so excited that he leaped out of the tub and ran down the street shouting, "Eureka!"

During the 1600's Renaissance scientists studied Archimedes' work. Although they found his calculations to be correct, they could not gather how he did them. Archimedes enjoyed teasing other mathematicians, so he gave clues about his methods but did not fully reveal them. Among his many discoveries were: laws of levers and pulleys, the center of gravity, a highly accurate catapult, and the Archimedean Screw which pulls water up out of a hole, and is still widely used today. Archimedes' mathematics remained a mystery until 1906 when Professor Johan Heiberg discovered a Christian prayer book in the ancient city of Constantinople. The book had been written in the thirteenth century on reused paper. Heiberg could make out traces of mathematics. The monks who wrote the prayer book had tried to remove the calculations. Historians revealed that it was actually an ancient copy Archimedes' work, now called the Archimedes Palimpsest.

Archimedes accurately calculated pi to nine decimal places. He was then able to find the volume of a sphere. He was so pleased with his work that he left instructions for this particular mathematical proof to be carved on his gravestone. When Archimedes was killed during a Roman conquest of Syracuse in 212 BC, his tomb was made in the shape of a sphere within a cylinder. Sadly, his tomb has been lost, along with much of his work.

("Archimedes." Famous Scientists. famousscientists.org. 1 Jul. 2014. Web. 4/7/2016).

HERNRI BRACONNOT

Henri Braconnot was born in Commercy, Germany in 1780. His father was a lawyer in the nearby town. When Henri was still a young boy, his father died, and his mother sent him and his younger brother to a strict boarding school. The corporal punishment used there did not inspire Henri to learn. He became so rebellious his mother was forced to move him to a less prestigious school. While Henri and his brother were away at school, his mother remarried a military doctor. This new stepfather wanted to get rid of the boys. So he sent 13 year old Henri away to the town of Nancy to be apprenticed in a pharmacy. Henri enjoyed learning pharmacology, chemistry, and botany there for two years. At age 15, he was drafted into army. This was an advantageous turn of events because it allowed him to travel around the country, where he took many classes and even learned how to play the guitar. When his time in the army ended, Henri went to Paris to study. He began doing research on a fossilized horn which had been found in a cave. He discovered that it contained calcium phosphate, many minerals, and gelatin. Up until this time, scientists believed that it was not possible to detect gelatin in a fossil. This revelation was the beginning of Henri's scientific research career and fame.

At age 22, he returned to Nancy, Germany. There, he was chairman of the local botanical garden. This position allowed him much freedom to pursue plant chemistry. He worked on plant extracts, plants acids, fats, and alkaloids. He even extracted sugar from beets and sawdust. It was during this time that he extracted fumaric acid and chitin from mushrooms. Over the years, Henri received many prestigious awards and appointments. He never married and always worked alone. Sadly, he suffered from stomach cancer. He had a poor opinion of doctors, and thus decided not to treat the cancer. He worked until his death in 1855.

(Nicklès J., Braconnot, His Life and Work, Mem. Acad. Stanislas, xxiiicxlix, 1855.) (Simonin F., Biography of M. Henri Braconnot, Compt. Rendus Trav. Soc. Méd. Nancy, 1834- 1855, p 51-79, 1856.) (François Th., Henry Braconnot, Oilseeds, p 11, 365-371, 1956.) (Labrude P., Becq C., The Pharmacist and Chemist, Henri Braconnot, Rev. Hist. Pharm., p 51, 61-78, 2003.)

GEORGE WASHINGTON CARVER

George Washington Carver was born in 1864 in Diamond, Missouri. No one knows his exact birthday because he was born a slave to the Carver family. It is thought that George's father was killed in a farming accident before George was born. His mother's name was Mary. Shortly after George was born, raiders stormed the Carver farm and kidnapped George and his mother. His mother died before she could be rescued, but his master traded a $300 race horse for the infant George and took him into his home. The Carvers taught George how to read and make simple herbal medicines. George was fascinated by plants. He did experiments with natural pesticides and various soils.

As a boy, local farmers called George the "plant doctor" and looked to him to improve their gardens. Despite many obstacles and deep-seated racism, George obtained a master's degree in agriculture. He accepted a job offer from Booker T. Washington and began work for the Tuskegee Institute in Alabama. George was resolute in his desire to help poor farmers. He introduced crop rotation using peanut plants by way of a horse drawn classroom. George invented approximately 300 different peanut products, from shaving cream to insulation, thus increasing the market demand for peanuts. Contrary to legend, George did not invent peanut butter. (That recipe is credited to the Incas in about 950 B.C.) George also worked with other plants and promoted legislation to help poor farmers. He died in 1943, leaving his life savings to found the George Washington Carver Institute for Agriculture.

(Bagley, Mary. LiveScience.com. George Washington Carver: Biography, Inventions & Quotes. December 6, 2013.)

George was never rich but was always humble. He gave God the glory for all of his accomplishments. He prayed over his plants and experiments. When George studied nature, he saw the work of God. He said, "Never since have I been without this consciousness of the Creator speaking to me...The out of doors has been to me more and more a great cathedral in which God could be continuously spoken to and heard from."

(Federer, W. J. 1994. America's God and Country Encyclopedia of Quotations. Coppell, TX: FAME Publishing, p 97.)

THOMAS ANDREW KNIGHT

Thomas Andrew Knight was born to a wealthy family in Ludlow, England in 1759. His father died when he as a young boy, but his older brother helped him by giving him a farm with greenhouses and, later, an entire castle. Knight received a first-class education, but he learned more by experiment and observation in his own garden. Knight recorded his results in letters which were sent to the Board of Agriculture which is how most of his work has been preserved. He worked to solve many practical farming problems in order to increase crop yield. For instance, he did research on how to build better greenhouses and control pests that destroy crops. His most famous experiments are on the geotropism of plants. Geotropism refers to how plants recognize gravity and send the roots down and the stem up. In one experiment, Knight eliminated the influence of gravity on seeds by attaching them to the rim of a vertical wheel which revolved continuously. As each plant grew, it directed its stem toward the center of the wheel, but when the stem passed the center, its growth turned back toward the center. The roots always grew away from the center of the wheel. Although Knight observed geotropism, he could not explain it. Charles Darwin later read and drew conclusions from Knight's papers. Knight was elected to the British Royal Society in 1805, and he was president of the London Horticultural Society until his death in 1838.

("Knight, Thomas Andrew." Complete Dictionary of Scientific Biography. 2008. Encyclopedia.com. 25 Apr. 2016)

Knight did not attend church, partially due to the rampant corruption in the Church of England at the time. However, he believed the ideologies of Christianity. He used Biblical principles as a test of truth, in life and in science. He gave extensively to charities, but always with humility and grace. He was a remarkable father and grandfather in the fact that no matter how busy he was, he always set aside his work to answer the questions and engage in the games of his children.

(Knight, Thomas Andrew. A selection from the physiological and horticultural papers. Longman, Orme, Brown, Green, and Longmans, 1841. Papers, p 71-73.)

ANTOINE LAVOISIER

Antoine Lavoisier was born the son of a wealthy lawyer in Paris in 1743. He went to law school as his father wanted, but he was fascinated with science. He passionately pursued science while leading a full social life. Lavoisier's work in geology received notice when he was only 25. He took a young wife, Marie-Anne, who became his scientific collaborator. Lavoisier accepted several political appointments, one of which was Commissioner of the Royal Gunpowder and Saltpeter Administration. He remodeled the laboratory and brought in fine young chemists for what was later dubbed the "Chemical Revolution." Thus, he improved the quality and quantity of gunpowder produced.

The most notable characteristic of Lavoisier's chemistry was how he always determined the weights of the reactants and products, even the gasses. Thus, he concluded that although the nature of the chemicals changed, the mass of the matter that entered the reaction equaled the mass of the matter that exited the reaction. This is the basis for the law of conservation of matter; matter cannot be created or destroyed, only change form.

Lavoisier took part in the liberating the common people from the oppression of the government in the French Revolution. He drew up many plans for change, including the metric system. Sadly, the French Revolution eventually turned on its own supporters, and Lavoisier was executed in 1794.

(Chemical Heritage Foundation. "Antione-Laurent Lavoisier", Chemistry in History. chemicalheritage.org. April 27, 2016.)

Lavoisier's family had a strong alliance with the Roman Catholic Church. Lavoisier wrote to a controversial English author, "You have done a noble thing in upholding revelation and the authenticity of the Holy Scripture, and it is remarkable that you are using for the defense precisely the same weapons which were once used for the attack."

(Catholic Online. "Antoine-Laurent Lavoisier", Catholic Encyclopedia. catholic.org/encyclopedia. April 27, 2016.)

JOHANN BENEDICT

Johann Benedict Listing was born in Germany in 1808, the only child of a poor Czech family. Listing showed great intelligence at an early age, so his education was funded by several sponsors. He was interested in math, science, and art. Listing even made money for his family by doing calligraphy at age thirteen. Listing's education continued to be funded by scholarships and benefactors through receiving his doctorate. After his graduation, he went on a trip with his geology professor to study volcanoes in Sicily. Listing was tasked with collecting data on terrestrial magnetism. While on this trip, he was recruited to teach mathematics in England. He later became a physics professor and began to study the human eye. He published the poplar book Beiträge zur Physiologischen Optik. (Contributions to Physiological Optics), which was filled with careful drawings.

He married a spendthrift woman, and their marriage was constantly plagued with financial problems. They had two daughters. It was during a time of dire bankruptcy that Listing discovered the Möbius band, independently of August Ferdinand Möbius. The church saved the family from complete bankruptcy. A friend arranged for the church to help with the debt in order to repay Listing for nursing him through a life threatening illness thirty years earlier. It was said that Listing was "... industrious and inquisitive, kind and helpful, gregarious and witty, good-natured to a degree, a true friend to many, and an enemy to none."

(E. Breitenberger, Johann Benedict Listing, in I.M. James (ed.), History of Topology (Amsterdam, 1999), p 909-924.)

MARTIN LUTHER

Martin Luther was born into a peasant family in Eisleben, Germany in 1483. His father was a copper miner, and wanted a better life for his son. So Luther began school at age seven and continued through receiving a Master of Arts to become a lawyer. However, in 1505, Luther was caught in a huge thunderstorm. When he feared for his life, he cried out, "Save me, St. Anne, and I'll become a monk!" The storm died down, and Luther kept his promise in hopes of finding eternal salvation. However, monastery life was difficult and disillusioning. Luther witnessed much immorality among the Roman Catholic priests. Trying to suppress his spiritual turmoil, Luther worked to earn a doctorate in theology. As he studied the Bible, he realized that the key to salvation was faith.

In 1517, the Pope announced new indulgences to build St. Peter's Basilica. Luther angrily nailed a list of 95 theses (complaints) on the chapel door. Luther actually hoped to begin a discussion about the problems in the church, but within two months copies of the Ninety-Five Theses spread throughout Europe. The pope ordered Luther to withdraw his statements, but Luther refused unless scripture could prove him wrong. He went on to say that the Pope did not have the exclusive right to interpret scripture, thus Luther was excommunicated from the Roman Catholic Church. He was called before the Diet of Worms, an assembly of questioning authorities, but Luther stood firm in his convictions. He was declared a "convicted heretic" and had to go into hiding. While secluded, he translated the New Testament into German for the ordinary people to read. This drastically changed how people related to their church leaders. Furthermore, Luther began to organize the new Lutheran Church. Luther settled down, married a former nun, and had six children.

(Biography.com Editors. "Martin Luther Biography" The Biography.com. A&E Television Networks. May 14, 2016)

JACK MINER

Jack Miner was born on April 10, 1865 in Ohio. Miner loved being outdoors. After he attended class for only three months, his teacher said he wasn't smart enough to go to school. Therefore, he spent his days happily playing in the woods. His father was a struggling brick maker. In an attempt to make more money, he moved the family to Ontario, Canada when Miner was thirteen years old. Miner began to hunt animals in the woods of Canada to provide food for his family. He was so successful that he became a market hunter, shooting and trapping more than is family needed and selling the extra. During this period of his life, he thoughtlessly slaughtered scores of animals for a profit. However, he began to see the numbers of marketable animals drop as they were hunted. He first changed from a market hunter to a sports hunter. Then he became a conservationist.

After four years of failure, Miner finally succeeded in attracting eleven of the remaining geese to a pond on his land. Soon thereafter, large flocks of water fowl began visiting his ponds regularly. Miner was curious about migration routes. After much trial and error, he captured four wild ducks and placed little metal bands (bracelets) on their feet. The bands had Miner's name and address and instructions to any hunter who killed the bird. The hunter was to write Miner a letter, telling him when and where the bird was shot. Miner also put a Bible verse on every bird and called them "missionary messengers." Using this method, he pioneered mapping migratory bird routes. He also began a lecturing campaign to educate people across North America. In 1904, he founded the Jack Miner Migratory Bird Sanctuary, which is still operational today. He helped establish the Migratory Bird Treaty Act of 1918, which helped protect the birds. Jack Miner died in 1944, having banded over 50,000 ducks and 40,000 geese. Miner's faith in God was the guiding force in his bird conversation.

He believed that humans are to play an active role in protecting the environment.

(Linton, James M., and Calvin W. Moore. The Story of Wild Goose Jack: The Life and Work of Jack Miner. Montréal: CBC Enterprises/Les Entreprises Radio-Canada, 1984. Print.)

AUGUST FERDINAND MÖBIUS

August Ferdinand Möbius was born in 1790 in Germany, an only child. His father taught dance. Unfortunately, his father died when Möbius was only three. His uncle stepped in to provide for the family. His mother homeschooled him until he was thirteen years old, at which time he went to college. He studied under several prominent professors, focusing on mathematics, astronomy, and topology. It was during this time he discovered the Möbius strip simultaneously with Johann Benedict Listing. He became a professor of astronomy and even oversaw construction of the university's new observatory. While he was working on a thesis about stars, the Prussian army held a draft. Möbius avoided the army and kept up his studies. Although his research was quite brilliant, he was not a very talented lecturer. Professors of that time were funded by paying students, not research grants. Möbius became so destitute, he advertised that his classes were free in order to attract students. Finally, his career began to improve, and Möbius became head of the observatory at Leipzig.

He took care of his aging mother. When she died, Möbius married and had three children. Although his wife went blind, she was an excellent mother. His sons and grandsons grew up to be quite brilliant and successful. He wrote many original works in mathematics and astronomy. He died at age seventy-eight, after teaching at Leipzig for fifty years.

("Möbius, August Ferdinand." Complete Dictionary of Scientific Biography. 2008.Encyclopedia.com. 26 May. 2016)

HAVE YOU TRIED BIG BIBLE SCIENCE BOOK 1?

BIG BIBLE  helps children and those who teach them to explore God's World and God's Word through real world science experiments. There are twenty-one different units taking students through scientific concepts such as Gravity, Friction, Animal Classification and the Nervous System. God creates young minds to ask questions and seek answers. This book is designed to stir the imaginations of students and develop a lasting love for Christ. The units are fun, interesting, and affirm the biblical worldview of creation. *Big Bible Science* is written to appeal to various ages and learning styles. This material is ideal for homeschoolers or classroom-based activities.

CHAPTER COMPONENTS:

	Objectives:	These are the science learning goals.
	Materials:	What you need before each lesson
	The Big Idea:	A scientific explanation of the lesson that also ties in a biblical perspective.
	Activities:	Demonstrations, games and experiments.
	Apply it:	Ideas about how to find examples of the lesson in your world.
	Go Beyond:	For more advanced students this will challenge them to think and experiment further.

EXPERIMENT UNITS INCLUDE: *Gravity, *Newton's First, Second and Third Laws of Motion, *Coefficient of Friction, *Static Electricity, *Acid Base Taste Test, *Combustion Reactions, * Plant Requirements, *Lunar Craters, *Water Cycle, *Angle of the Sun's Rays, *Basic Animal Classification, *Field Trip: The Zoo, *Nervous System, *Muscles, *Bones, *Respiratory System, *Circulatory System, *Digestive System, *Urinary System

"*Big Bible Science* is for the head and the heart: a good mix of solid science and inspirational devotions. It's straight-forward, relevant, accurate and God-glorifying, great for kids and teachers." —Amy McFarlance, Homeschooling Parent

ERIN LEE GREEN is originally from Arkansas she now lives in Puerto Rico. She taught chemistry, astronomy and geology at public school after having gained a Master of Arts in teaching. And now enjoys sharing the wonders of God's world and salvation through homeschooling her own children.

EXPERIMENT CHECKLIST

Potential & Kinetic Energy

- [ ] Slide
- [ ] Swing
- [ ] Spring Rider
- [ ] Energy from God

Simple Machines on a Playground

- [ ] Simple Machine Hunt
- [ ] God's Blessing Jar

Mechanical Advantage of a Lever

- [ ] Heavy Lifting
- [ ] Balancing Penny Act
- [ ] Seesaw Opposites

Fixed Pulley: Changing the Direction of Force

- [ ] Build a Simple Fixed Pulley
- [ ] Saul's Life Changes Direction
- [ ] Movable Pulley Tug-of-war

Angular Momentum and Centripetal Motion

- [ ] Swing and Angular Momentum
- [ ] Inertia
- [ ] Centripetal Motion
- [ ] God's love Mobius circle

Buoyancy of Boats

- [ ] Water Displacement
- [ ] Boat Float
- [ ] Sink the Boat
- [ ] In the Boat with Jesus

Law of Conservation of Matter

- [ ] The Giant Oak
- [ ] Production of a Gas
- [ ] Jesus Feeds 5000

Indications of a Chemical Reaction

- [ ] Plaster of Paris
- [ ] Candle
- [ ] Baking Soda and Vinegar
- [ ] Clean a Penny
- [ ] Hydrogen Peroxide and Yeast
- [ ] Blind Faith

Heat Capacity and Specific Heat

- [ ] Heat Capacity
- [ ] Specific Heat
- [ ] Hot Chocolate

Condensation

- [ ] Bottle in a Bag
- [ ] Cup Trap

Colligative Properties

- [ ] Freezing Point Depression
- [ ] Freezing Point Elevation

Symmetry in Nature

- [ ] Linear Symmetry Butterfly
- [ ] Radial Symmetry Flowers
- [ ] Nature Walk

Deciduous and Evergreen Trees

- [ ] Righteous Tree
- [ ] Tree Identification

Plant a Bean

- [ ] Bean Sprouting
- [ ] Sensing Gravity
- [ ] Rooted in His Love

Parts of a Plant at the Dinner Table

- [ ] Study the Food
- [ ] Prepare and Eat the Food

Symbiosis

- [ ] Love Notes
- [ ] Matching Hints
- [ ] Nature Walk

Bird Population Study

- [ ] Build a Bird Feeder
- [ ] Bird Craft: "More Valuable than They"
- [ ] Bird Count
- [ ] Bar Graph

Endoskeleton versus Exoskeleton

- [ ] Search for Creatures
- [ ] God's Creatures
- [ ] Nature Walk

Carnivores, Herbivores, & Omnivores:

- [ ] The Food Chain
- [ ] Compare and Contrast
- [ ] Food Chain
- [ ] Food Web

How the Moon Shines

- [ ] Lunar Reflection
- [ ] Lunar Reflection Lost-and-Found
- [ ] Light of the World, Reflecting Jesus' Light

Weathering & Erosion

- [ ] Mechanical Weathering by Pressure
- [ ] Mechanical Weathering by Freezing Expansion
- [ ] Chemical Weathering by Acid
- [ ] Erosion by Wind
- [ ] Erosion by Water, Particle Size Comparison

Page(s)	Experiment	Image where attribution is required	Attribution
14-17	Exp. 1	Background - Water	Photo by Sakura on Unsplash
17	Exp. 1	Dam	Photo by Lode Lagrainge on Unsplash
18-20	Exp. 2	Background - Nails	Photo by Clint Bustrillos on Unsplash
18-20	Exp. 2	Polaroid - pulley	Photo by Brett Jordan on Unsplash
21-25	Exp. 3	Paper Clip	CCO Public Domain
26-31	Exp. 4	Background - rope	Photo by Tim Boote on Unsplash
26-31	Exp. 4	Polaroid - Cable Car	Photo by Aditya Chinchure on Unsplash
32-35	Exp. 5	Background - lights motion	Photo by Kinson Leung on Unsplash
32-35	Exp. 5	Polaroid - Ice sakter	Photo by Rod Long on Unsplash
36-39	Exp. 6	Polaroid - paper boat	Photo by Aartak Petrosyan on Unsplash
40-43	Exp. 7	Pic - Antoine Lavoisier	Jacques-Louis David [Public domain]
48-50	Exp. 9	Polaroid - Hot choc	Photo by Anna Onishchuk on Unsplash
51-53	Exp. 10	Background - Condensation	Photo by Wenniel Lun on Unsplash
56-59	Exp. 11	Globe	Photo by Andrew Neel from Pexels
60-62	Exp. 11	kaleidoscope	Photo by Malcolm Lightbody on Unsplash
63-67	Exp. 13	Polaroid - trees	Photo by Arnaud Mesureur on Unsplash
66	Exp. 13	Larch Leaves	Larch Needles from Max Pixel
66	Exp. 13	Holly Leaves	Photo by Annie Spratt on Unsplash
67	Exp. 13	Pic - Colourful trees	Photo by Aaron Burden on Unsplash
68-71	Exp. 14	Background - soil and seedlings	Photo by Markus Spiske on Unsplash
72-74	Exp. 15	Background - Cabbage leaves	Photo by Bailey Heedick on Unsplash
74	Exp. 15	Strawberry Plant	Strawberry plant image by OpenClipart-Vectors from Pixabay
75-78	Exp. 16	Background - Fur	Photo by Erol Ahmed on Unsplash
77	Exp. 16	Sea Anemone	Image by LoggaWiggler from Pixabay
77	Exp. 16	Shark	Photo by Katerina Kerdi on Unsplash
77	Exp. 16	Remora	NOAA CCMA Biogeography Team [Public domain]
77	Exp. 16	Yucca Moth	Judy Gallagher [Creative Commons CC BY-SA 2.0]
77	Exp. 16	Yucca plant	Photo by Jim Rhoades on Unsplash
77	Exp. 16	Honey Guide Bird	Steve Garvie, Dunfermline, Fife, Scotland [Creative Commons CC BY-SA 2.0]
77	Exp. 16	Honey badger	Wiki Commons CC BY 3.0
77	Exp. 16	Oxpecker	Image by Taryn Scholtz from Pixabay
77	Exp. 16	Crocodile	Photo by Kyaw Tun on Unsplash
77	Exp. 16	Egyptian Plover	Steve Garvie, Dunfermline, Fife, Scotland [Creative Commons CC BY-SA 2.0]
77	Exp. 16	Butterfly	Image by Desha from Pixabay
77	Exp. 16	Wrasse Cleaner	Rickard Zerpe [Creative Commons CC BY 2.0]
77	Exp. 16	Eel	Photo by Wouter Naert on Unsplash
79-81	Exp. 17	Background - Seagulls	Photo by Fabiana Rizzi on Unsplash
79-81	Exp. 17	Polaroid - Parrott	Photo by David Clode on Unsplash
80	Exp. 17	Bird Feeder	Photo by Annie Spratt on Unsplash
82-84	Exp. 18	Background - Jellyfish	Photo by Tony Reid on Unsplash
82-84	Exp. 18	Polaroid - Skeleton	Photo by Mathew Schwartz on Unsplash
85-91	Exp. 19	Background - Sevannah	Photo by elCarito on Unsplash
88, 90	Exp. 19	Caribou	Free vector art via Vecteezy
88, 90	Exp. 19	Wolf	Free vector art via Vecteezy
88, 90	Exp. 19	Grasshopper	Free vector art via Vecteezy
92-95	Exp. 20	Background - Luna surface	Photo by NASA on Unsplash
92-95	Exp. 20	Polaroid - Moon	Photo by Ganapathy Kumar on Unsplash
93	Exp. 20	Teddy	Photo by Sandy Millar on Unsplash
96-100	Exp. 21	Background - sandstone erosion	Photo by Sven van der Pluijm on Unsplash
96-100	Exp. 21	Polaroid - Sand castle	Photo by Dallas Reedy on Unsplash
99	Exp. 21	Grand Canyon - errosion	Photo by Gert Boers on Unsplash
99	Exp. 21	Statue	Photo by Zac Farmer on Unsplash
100	Exp. 21	Sinkhole lake	Photo by Katerina Kerdi on Unsplash
100	Exp. 21	Sinkhole Car	Photo SANY0012 Charlie, Flickr

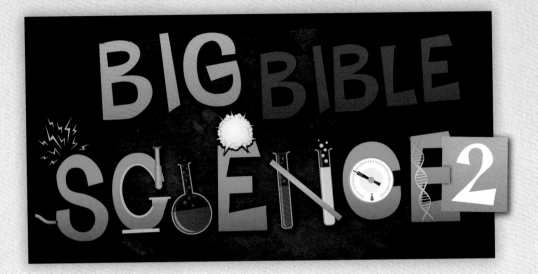

Christian Focus Publications publishes books for adults and children under its four main imprints: Christian Focus, CF4K, Mentor and Christian Heritage.

CHRISTIAN FOCUS PUBLICATIONS

Christian Focus   **Christian Heritage**   **CF4K**   **Mentor**

Our books reflect our conviction that God's Word is reliable and Jesus is the way to know him, and live forever with him.

Our children's publication list includes a Sunday School curriculum that covers pre-school to early teens, and puzzle and activity books. We also publish personal and family devotional titles, biographies and inspirational stories that children will love.

If you are looking for quality Bible teaching for children then we have an excellent range of Bible stories and age-specific theological books.

From pre-school board books to teenage apologetics, we have it covered!

Find us at our web page: www.christianfocus.com